The Friends of the Pang, Kennet ℰ

AROUND
THE VALLEY
OF THE
PANG

An exploration of the Pang Valley
in West Berkshire

Dick Greenaway

Drawings by Dorcas Ward

With a chapter on the river by Ben McFarland

Dedicated to

Margot and Richard Walker
of Ashampstead Green
with deep respect
and great affection.

Around the Valley of the Pang:

An Exploration of the Pang Valley in West Berkshire.

Text and illustrations, except Chapter 8 and as acknowledged,
copyright © Dick Greenaway 2007

Chapter headers and frontispiece copyright © Dorcas Ward 2007

Text and illustrations Chapter 8 copyright © Ben McFarland 2007

ISBN 978-09543597-2-0

Design and origination: *Magenta Graphics*. Project management: *Intaglio*.
Printed in Great Britain: *ESP Colour Ltd*.

Published by: The Friends of the Pang, Kennet and Lambourn Valleys,
The Old Estate Office, Englefield Road, Theale, Reading RG7 5DZ.

ACKNOWLEDGEMENTS

On behalf of the Friends of the Pang, Kennet and Lambourn Valleys we
would like to thank the following donors,
without whose generous help the production of this book
would not have been possible:

Sir William Benyon and the Englefield Charitable Trust

Mr Terry Crawford

Lord Iliffe of Yattendon

The Gerald Palmer Eling Trust

The Well Barn Estate

The income resulting from the sale of this book will go to supporting the
work of the Pang, Kennet and Lambourn Valleys Project FWAG. The Project
helps farmers and landowners in the valleys to farm and manage their land
in an environmentally sensitive manner for the benefit of both the wildlife
and the man-made heritage.

We are deeply in debt to Richard and Margot Walker for their professional
skill, for the encouragement they have given and for the hours they have
spent reading and commenting on the manuscript. We could not have done
without them.

Our thanks also to Professor Peter Worsley for commenting on the geology
and to Jill Greenaway for commenting on the history and archaeology. As
always any errors or omissions are ours.

We would like to acknowledge the excellent service that the Berkshire
Record Office has provided to us over many years and also the help and
information on World War 2 weapons and fortifications we received from
'Fire Power', the Royal Artillery Museum. We also thank the East Ilsley Local
History Society for their help and for the loan of documents.

The majority of photographs are from the Greenaway Collection of Modern
and Historic Photographs of the Pang Valley. The illustrations in chapter
eight were provided by Ben McFarland. Other pictures and images are
acknowledged individually.

Historic photographs pass through many hands over the years and we
have done our best to trace the copyright owner in all cases. If we have
infringed anyone's copyright we offer our apologies.

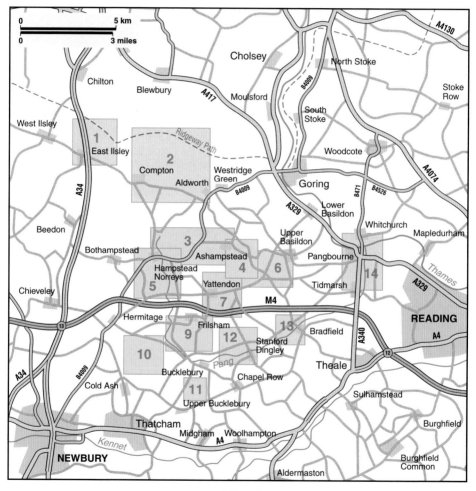

CONTENTS

INTRODUCTION

It is possible to know an area at many different levels. At the most superficial level one could claim to know the Pang Valley simply by being able to drive from one village to another without having to use a map. At a less superficial level a knowledge of the Rights of Way, sufficient to allow one to go for a lengthy walk confident that one would not get lost, would support a claim to know the Valley. But to *really know* an area we believe it is necessary to try to *understand why* the path is there, *why* it bends at that spot, *why* its hedges have the plants that they do, *why* there is a wood here rather than there, *what* the wood was used for, what plants and animals live in it, *why* the village or the farm developed as it did. Even a small area like our valley will provide a lifetime of enquiry and delight in solving only a few of the puzzles. Our experience is that as the knowledge grows so does the love and the sense of belonging to the landscape. The place ceases to be impersonal and becomes home.

*   *   *

The Friends of the Pang, Kennet and Lambourn Valleys are a gathering of people who feel passionate about the valleys and in the years 2001 and 2002 they ran a campaign to raise awareness of the richness of the natural and man made environment of the Pang Valley in particular. The campaign culminated in October 2002 with the publication of 'In the Valley of the Pang' and a series of exhibitions in Newbury Museum and various Pang Valley village halls. The book was a great success and sold out within four months.

As part of the campaign The Friends ran a series of monthly 'lecture walks' at different locations in the Valley. The walks were guided by someone with local knowledge of the route and for some walks we involved a local farmer or forester to explain about the area and the activities observed during the walk. Walkers were provided with leaflets so that they could repeat the walk more informally. Each leaflet contained a map of the walk with notes on the history and wildlife of the area. These walks were very popular and many people returned for successive walks. It seemed a waste not to use the information that had been gathered and there was an obvious interest amongst walkers for a 'walks book' which provided more than just a simple 'turn left, turn right, climb over the stile ...' set of instructions. So The Friends decided to publish a companion book to 'In the Valley of the Pang' which would contain the collected leaflets with additional information on each area. This book is the result.

*   *   *

The book is designed to be read as a book in its own right – whether the walks are explored on the ground or not. It is designed to be dipped into, rather than to be read from cover to cover. Each chapter discusses the history and wildlife of a different part of the Valley. The two are inseparable. The trees and plants are there as a result of human actions or lack of action and it is not possible to understand the wildlife without considering the human history, nor the human history without considering the wildlife.

Since the River Pang runs through the whole length we have provided a single, more detailed, chapter on the river and its wildlife. This allows us to avoid tedious repetition every time a chapter includes the river.

We have decided that some repetition is acceptable and necessary. Information in the general section of each chapter is sometimes repeated in the detailed notes provided for the walk and in other chapters. To do otherwise would have involved the reader in regularly referring backwards and forwards and this would be tedious and distracting. The pages of walk notes are tinted to make them obviously different from the general sections.

* * *

The walks vary in length from a couple of miles to a nine mile trek across the downs. A careful map based on the 1:25,000 Ordnance Survey map is provided for each walk which will be adequate for most purposes but we recommend that a copy of the relevant Ordnance Survey 'Explorer' map be used in conjunction with our map and in each case we quote its number. Where the route is particularly difficult to follow we have added detailed instructions. All the walks are on Public Rights of Way, on Permitted Paths or – as in the case of the Eling Estate – on paths which landowners have opened to walkers.

* * *

We have provided notes on the hazards which may be encountered on each walk, but we cannot be responsible for explorers' personal safety.

* * *

Car parking can sometimes be a problem. Whenever possible we have started our walks near a place where parking is accepted, such as village hall car parks or village side roads. This has not always been possible and we would ask walkers to park with care so as not to obstruct roads or field gates.

* * *

Somewhere in each chapter we refer to the various Periods of Antiquity - 'Mesolithic', 'Neolithic' etc. The normal convention is to quote the date range after each one every time it is used. This we find to be clumsy and to interrupt the flow of the narrative. Therefore :-

Mesolithic (Middle Stone Age)	c.10,000BC	to	c.4,000BC
Neolithic (New Stone Age)	c.4,000BC	to	c.2,500BC
Bronze Age	c.2,500BC	to	c.750BC
Iron Age	c.750BC	to	43AD
Roman Period	43AD	to	5th century AD
Early Medieval (Saxon Period)	5th century AD	to	1066AD
Medieval Period	1066AD	to	c.1500AD
The Norman Conquest	was in 1066		
Domesday Book	was compiled in 1086		

These are not hard and fast dates and frequently change as archaeologists make new discoveries, but they will provide an adequate framework for our chapters. Periods tended to overlap and fade into each other. There would still have been people living in a Neolithic way and using stone tools long after bronze was discovered and the Saxon way of life for the majority of ordinary people survived for many years after the Norman Conquest in 1066.

*   *   *

With all that said, we hope you enjoy our book and that your delight in this most fascinating valley is increased by our efforts.

Dick Greenaway   Dorcas Ward   Ben McFarland
Ashampstead Common   *Frilsham*

CHAPTER ONE

Sheep Fairs & Chalk Downs ~ The Top End

East Ilsley duck pond

Let us start our exploration of the valley where the river starts – on the high chalk downs. The downs are the nearest we have to the wild moorlands and uplands of the north and west and they evoke similar responses. There is something pagan about the atmosphere of the chalk downs. Perhaps it is their bare skylines and landscapes uncluttered with fussy vegetation. Perhaps it is the positioning of the farms and villages in hollows and valleys, sheltered and hidden by the smooth ridges. Perhaps the pagan ambiance is caused by the multitude of prehistoric remains, for if the lower valley with its early churches and ancient manors is a medieval landscape, the downland is definitely prehistoric.

The Geology of the Chalk Downs. Chalk is a limestone which was deposited in a warm shallow sea 100 to 70 million years ago. It is mainly composed of coccoliths which are microscopic plates from the skeletons of plankton. It also contains the remains of larger creatures, such as sea urchins and sponges, as fossils. The sediment settled as mud and was converted into rock by intense pressure over immense periods of time.

The mud also contained silica from the skeletons of other marine creatures. The flints in the chalk are formed when the silica is leached from the mud and re-deposited in the hollows left by decayed sea bed plants and animal remains and within burrow cavities.

The dry valleys were carved out by melt water while the chalk was frozen at the end of several Ice Ages. This allowed the water to flow over the surface rather than sinking into the chalk. A high water table may have allowed the erosion to continue after the frozen chalk melted.

The River Pang is a *bourne*. This means that for quite lengthy periods it can be dry. The chalk acts like a sponge and soaks up rain. Long periods of rain raise the level of the water within the chalk and allow springs to flow further and further up the valley as the groundwater rises. Conversely a long dry period or over abstraction lowers the groundwater and the upper channel dries. The *perennial* head is at the Blue Pools below Stanford Dingley and below this the river never fails.

There are two sources for the Pang. The western branch rises in or above East Ilsley pond and the northern branch rises on Churn Plain and flows south along the line of the old railway. Although now almost insignificant, it once provided enough water to power a small water mill. The two streams join at Compton and then flow south together.

The History of the Downland. The Downs were colonised by trees after the end of the last Ice Age (c.10,000BC). Clearing was begun by the first farmers during the Neolithic Period. They have been largely treeless ever since. There are monuments of all periods. There is a Neolithic Long Barrow on Sheep Down, now visible only as a soil mark, and the remains of prehistoric and Roman fields can be seen everywhere, particularly in damp weather after ploughing. Iron Age Hill forts line the crest of the Downs and Roman pottery is picked up in many fields. During the medieval period and later they were particularly important for sheep

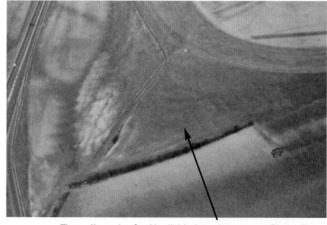

The soil mark of a Neolithic long barrow on Sheep Down

grazing. They have been ploughed at many periods, most recently after the Napoleonic Wars and since about 1970. It is likely that large areas will revert to grassland in the near future as the new farming regime makes their use for cereal growing unprofitable. However, the demand for energy crops such as oil seed rape and elephant grass may keep them as arable.

East Ilsley village and church. East Ilsley is surrounded by archaeological features going back to the Neolithic Period. The village sits in a sheltered hollow and the pond is probably an enlarged spring and thus a reliable source of water. It is likely that people have lived on the site of the village for at least 5,000 years.

The church was built in the 13th century but a church is mentioned in Domesday Book so this is not the first church on the site. The humps and bumps in the paddock next to the church may be its remains or the remains of medieval houses. The tower was rebuilt in 1625 and extensive alterations were carried out in 1845.

The East Ilsley Sheep Fairs. Fairs were the Shopping Centres of the medieval period. They were held under license from the king and were a major financial benefit to the lord of a manor who could impose rents and tolls on traders and whose court would collect fines from miscreants. As the towns grew they gradually took over many of the supply functions of fairs which then became more associated with the sale of agricultural produce. Nevertheless, by the end of the 15th century about 1500 fairs were still being held annually in England. East Ilsley's Fair was established under a charter granted by Henry III (1216-72) and a second charter was granted in 1620 by

The Sheep Fair. Pen Meadow
© *English Heritage National Monuments Record*

James I. Initially the fair was held weekly, but was later reduced to about 14 per year. In addition to sheep, cattle and wheat were also traded and itinerant traders would have brought pottery, clothes and other domestic items. The opening of the Kennet and Avon Canal in 1795 drew away the wheat trade and the fairs finally ceased in 1934.

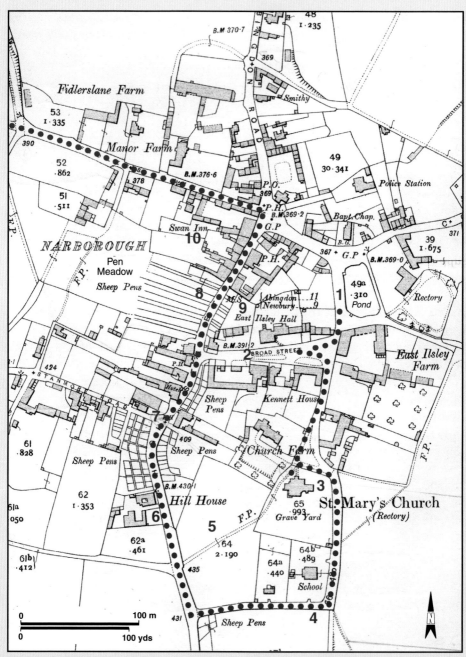

East Ilsley village

Based on the Ordnance Survey map of 1911

This walk includes
East Ilsley village and The Ridgeway. It starts and finishes at East Ilsley Pond.

- **It is about 5 miles or 8 km long. The route is along wide, clear and well marked tracks.**
- **There is one short hill and two long hills on this walk and surfaces can be uneven and muddy.**
- **The Ridgeway area is exposed and can be wild in bad weather.**
- **Part of the route uses a busy road without pavements.**

Ordnance Survey map Explorer 170 'Abingdon, Wantage & Vale of the White Horse' will be useful.

1. The pond. This is certainly artificial and was dug to store water from the springs which flow from the chalk. It would have been the main water supply for both animals and people for many centuries, supplemented by wells. It is also the head of the western branch of the River Pang but this only flows when prolonged wet weather has raised the water table.

2. Broad Street. Kennet House is much older than its late 17th century false front indicates. It was named after its owner Charles Kennet who was once mayor of London. In the early 19th century it was a girls boarding school and had 19 pupils in 1841. Note the three fire marks. These indicate the insurance companies covering the building. The Hall, on the other side of the road, was a boys school at the same time.

3. The church. The church is thought to have been built in 1240. The tower was rebuilt in 1625 . The date is on the arch. The north aisle was added in 1845. Look for the carvings on the pillars. These may be the wool marks of rich graziers who contributed to the cost of building the original church. Look also for the strange carving near the entrance to the rood screen gallery. The rood screen was probably removed in the mid 17th century immediately before or soon after the Civil War and the execution of Charles I. The little basin is a holy water stoop. The pulpit is Jacobean.

This is probably a grazier's wool mark

A family's numbered pew   Scratch dials to time the sermon

Note the numbered pews. These were exclusive to individual families who paid rent for them.

On the outside of the church, on the corner stonework, there are scratch dials which allowed the priest's assistant to time the sermons!

The East Ilsley Local History Society have calculated that, since 1608, about 2850 people have been buried in the church yard. As it became filled additional layers of soil have been added thus raising the surface to its present level.

4. The Butts. Butts Corner and Narrow Lane mark the site of the archery practice ground. From at least the 13th century, archery after church was compulsory in order to supply skilled archers for the army

5. Deserted site. The humps and holloways in this paddock may be the remains of old buildings.

6. High Street. Until 1966 this was the A34. Its steepness and narrowness led to many bizarre accidents. On one occasion a milk lorry filled a cellar with milk! The road was lined with pens for the sheep fairs.

7. Pubs. The village is well blessed with pubs but when it had the sheep markets there were several more. They were the meeting places of sellers and buyers and they fed and housed the shepherds, drovers and carters who attended the market. Market days were often very drunken affairs.

8. Sheep pens. As can be seen from the map, pens for sheep and cattle were erected alongside the street. Pen Meadow was the main site and the ridges and hollows are the result of centuries of wear. So many sheep were traded that it was claimed boys could run on the backs of the sheep from the outside of the village to the centre without touching the ground.

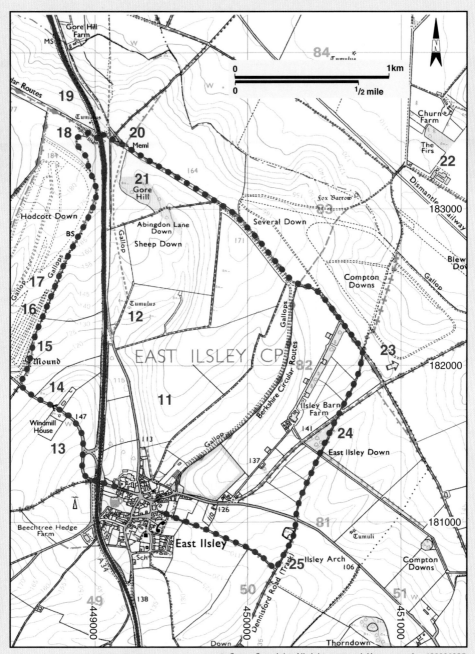

9. Market memorial. Note the piece of local sarsen and the plaque which commemorates the markets. Note also the milestone with its date of 1776. This was erected by a Turnpike Trust. No engineered roads were constructed in the thirteen hundred years after the Roman Period and medieval roads were simple tracks. Turnpike Trusts were formed to take over a route. They built and maintained a road and charged tolls for its use. The route of the turnpike can be traced by looking for standard pattern milestones. (See chapter 14)

The Milestone

10. Swan Inn. This was a coaching inn. It catered for travellers on the important north-south road which later became the A34. It also served the market and was the venue for other local business. The Enclosure Commissioners who decided on the enclosure of the common lands of Compton met here.

11. Prehistoric fields. Again only visible as soil marks. The grid of faint light coloured lines on the eastern slope are the banks around prehistoric fields. Some fields of this type were in use throughout the Roman Period, a life of two or three thousand years.

12. Neolithic long barrow. This lay on the eastern side of the valley. It has been ploughed flat, but a soil mark can still be seen after ploughing particularly in damp weather.

13. The windmill. The village windmill stood just behind the house.

14. Strip lynchets. These steps are caused by the ploughing of strips along the hillside. The loosened soil moved down hill away from the upper boundary and collected against the lower one. They were probably created between 1000 and 1348 when the population outgrew food supply and farmers were forced to use marginal land. The Black Death in 1348/9 drastically reduced the population and the marginal areas were abandoned.

15. The Wheat Road. This track is also the parish boundary. In this area parish boundaries were established in the 9th century. They often followed the boundaries of existing estates which can sometimes be traced even further back in history. The track is therefore at least a thousand years old, and probably very much older.

16. Racehorse gallops. This smooth grass swathe is a training track. The dry even turf attracted horse trainers from the 18th century. The Duke of Northumberland had stables at Kate's Gore in 1764. Charles II set rules for racing to encourage the breeding of stronger horses to improve the army's

Silverweed

Yellow toadflax

cavalry. Steeplechasing started later in the mid-1800's. The close mowing of the gallops has produced a valuable and distinctive flora which is now threatened by the introduction of engineered 'all-weather' tracks.

17. Chalkland plants. The centuries of grazing impoverished the thin soils. This, plus the existence of some areas of acid soils, has produced a distinctive flora. Silverweed roots and leaves were boiled and eaten. Travellers lined their shoes with silverweed leaves to ease tired feet. Yarrow and mugwort were used to flavour beer. Look for: plantains, purple knapweed, white campion, salad burnet, wild marjoram, wild carrot, St John's wort, mignonette, and yellow toadflax. You will find many more as the seasons change.

18. The Ridgeway. This is a National Long Distance Trail running from Norfolk to Stonehenge. It has acquired its own mythology and is claimed as a Neolithic Road and the oldest road in Britain.

This image is mainly the product of 19th century surveyors. It often does not appear on old maps and in places it runs over fields in use during the Iron Age and Roman periods Their ditches can be seen in the side ditch east of Point 20.

19. View north. The Rutherford Laboratory was formerly Atomic Research Station Harwell sited on a WW2 airfield. The distant ridge is an old coral reef. The double hill is an Iron Age fort.

20. Lifeguard memorial. Marks a 1947 army training accident. Look for the dark profiles of ancient field ditches in the north boundary ditch.

The Lifeguard Stone

21. Poors Furze. This was an area of common woodland where fuel could be gathered

22. Churn Basin. The north branch of the Pang rises here. This col provides a natural route over the high chalk ridge. It is followed by the old railway from Didcot to Southampton. During the Boer War a firing range was established here for long distance shooting and this was re-used for training in both World Wars.

23. Lowbury Hill. The hill to the east near the Ridgeway was the site of a Roman temple. The hill gets its name from a Saxon barrow *(low)* + enclosure – the temple ruins - *(burgh)*. (See Chapter 2)

24. Danes Spear Road. Also called *Danesford Road* supposedly from the Battle of Ashdown but more probably from a 19th century antiquarian's imagination!

25. River Pang. The course crosses here and runs to Compton. During the winter of 2000-01 the river flowed strongly and formed a large lake in the field to the east. Many valley villages were flooded by groundwater from Christmas until March.

Sources and further reading

Victoria County History – Berkshire

Rowley & Wood	*Deserted Villages* – Shire Archaeology 1982
Boyd D	*The Running Horses – a brief history of racing in Berkshire from 1740.* Berkshire County Libraries 1978
McMahon & Mankin	*The Story of Compton* Compton Parish Council 2000
Williamson T	*Shaping Medieval Landscapes* Windgather Press 2003
Mabey R	*Flora Britannica* London 1997
Greenaway & Ward (eds)	*In the Valley of the Pang* Friends of the Pang & Kennet Valleys 2002
Dyer J	*Southern England-an Archaeological Guide* Faber & Faber 1973
Morris J (Ed)	*Domesday Book – Berkshire.* Phillimore 1979
Ekwall E	*The Concise Oxford Dictionary of English Place-names.* Oxford 1974
Wilson J	*East Ilsley. Photographic Memories 1900 1970.* Privately published 1998

CHAPTER TWO

Downs, Temple and Bell
Exploring the watershed and the upper valley

Place Names. We accept place names as a given. They are simply a sound which is used to identify a location or a settlement. But think about it. When we give a place a new name it tends to be either an indication of ownership or a physical description. *Joe's Place* or *The Primrose Patch*. Our ancestors were no different and we can learn a lot about their countryside from the names they gave it. Compton, for instance, comes from the Old English words *cumb* and *tun; narrow valley* and *settlement in an enclosure. Valley Village* is a good description when you see the village from the surrounding hills. However, be warned! It is not quite that simple. The obvious meaning is not always the correct one and the earliest recorded version of the name should always be used.

Early History. There have been people living in the area since at least the Bronze Age and the sites of their burial mounds are scattered across the landscape. Sadly most of them have been ploughed flat. There was an extensive settlement in the Roman Period with a thriving pottery industry at Woodrows Farm, a burial site on Roden Down and a sacred site on Lowbury Hill. The fields outlined by the eroded banks and terraces at Streatley Warren were being worked in the Iron Age and in the Roman Period and there are traces of other boundaries all over the chalk. These are now visible only from the air as soil marks or as faint dark lines after the land has been ploughed and prepared for sowing. Grim's Ditch runs east to west across the high chalk and again can only be seen as a soil mark for most of its length. This is probably a tribal or estate boundary and dates from the Late Iron Age.

The Hundred of the Naked Thorn. Late Saxon society was well organised, well disciplined and literate. It was probably the most advanced society in northern Europe and this contributed to its downfall in 1066. The Norman invaders were able to grasp the key posts in the organisation and take over the running of the country with relatively little opposition. There was local resistance in the north, in East Anglia and along the Welsh border, but these were dealt with ruthlessly and in less than a generation the take-over was secure. The system of administration was based on the *Shire* with its *Shire Reeve* (sheriff). Central government (the king) sent writs, requiring a particular action, to the sheriff who carried out the instruction. The shire was divided into smaller units called *hundreds.* These had a local council which met regularly, usually in the open air, to discuss local problems, apportion tax demands and levy troop requirements for the king's army. To day's walk is through the Hundred of *Nachededorn* or Naked Thorn. This is thought to refer to the naked thorn around which King Alfred fought the decisive battle of Ashdown against the Danes in 871 AD. The battle was somewhere on the downs but the site has never been positively identified.

Domesday Book. In 1086 William the Conqueror ordered a survey of all the estates of his chief tenants. The survey was intended to define who held what land and on what terms. It recorded the value for taxation purposes of each holding. William wanted to know the value of the land he had conquered. The survey was completed in the amazingly short time of twelve months and is the primary document for local history in the southern part of England.

Like other ancient documents it must be used with care. For a start, it records manors, not parishes. Sometimes these coincide, but often there is more than one manor in a parish and manors often straddle parish boundaries. Compton is an example; there were two manors held by different tenants. Areas of arable land are given in terms of *land for ... ploughs* and areas of woodland as *woodland for ... pigs*. These terms have to be translated with care and historians have argued about their meaning for generations.

West Compton Manor House

Compton and Aldworth. Compton as already mentioned, had two manors, East and West Compton. Its more sheltered position and a water supply from the River Pang allowed a larger population. There were about thirty-one tenant families and eight slaves working about 450 acres of arable and 4 acres of meadow with, of course, extensive grazing on the downs. The river was strong enough to power a water mill.

Aldworth, like Compton, is an ancient settlement. Its name means *old enclosure* or *old homestead* in Early English. Thus it was already an ancient place when it was first recorded as *Aldewurde* in 1167. Domesday Book calls it *Elleorde* and lists *land for five ploughs ... woodland for ten pigs.* This may mean about 150 acres of arable and very little woodland to support ten tenant families and four slaves. Although not recorded, there would have been extensive grazing on the open down land.

Compton Manor House in 1720

This walk includes Compton Village, The Ridgeway and Aldworth Village. It starts and finishes at Compton Village Hall car park.

- It is about 9 miles or 14 km long. The route is along wide, clear and well marked tracks.
- There is a steady climb up to the Ridgeway and surfaces can be uneven and muddy.
- The Ridgeway area is exposed and can be wild in bad weather.
- Horses and riders may be encountered.

Ordnance Survey maps Explorer 170 'Abingdon, Wantage and Vale of the White Horse', and Explorer 158 'Newbury and Hungerford' will be useful.

Guidance note: Turn west (right) along Burrell Road to the T junction and turn north (right) to the next junction where you will see the Manor ahead of you. To reach Point 2, turn right and take the first turning on the left.

1. West Compton Manor House. Probably 15th century in origin. The ditch on the south side of the road is the Western Pang. The Research Centre was set up in 1937.

2. The Foundry. Like the foundry at Bucklebury, Baker's Foundry (The Whitewall Ironworks) started in the early 1800's making agricultural equipment – ploughs, carts, shepherds huts etc. They even made a bicycle! It was taken over by British Hoist & Crane in 1953 and closed in 1983. It is now Whitewalls Close.

3. Roden House. Originally 'Stokes Manor'. Probably 16th century in origin. In 1779 King George hunted a stag from Windsor and caught it in the hall of Roden House. It was kept at Compton until recovered and then hunted to Hurley. It was spared and named 'Compton'. The low walled area in front is probably the mill pond. Note the hand made bricks showing the dents made by stacking the wet clay blocks to dry and the colours and glazing caused by the variable heat in the stack's ducts. (See Chapter 9)

4. The Railway. The 'Didcot Newbury & Southampton Junction Railway' was built between 1879 and 1882 and absorbed by the Great Western Railway in 1923. During both World Wars it carried heavy traffic from the Midlands to the South Coast ports. It was doubled in 1943 and closed in 1964

5. The Slad. This was carved out by the vast flows of water and ice at the ends of the last few Ice Ages. The North Pang rises in the col to the north and follows the railway. The Slad forms a natural north – south route.

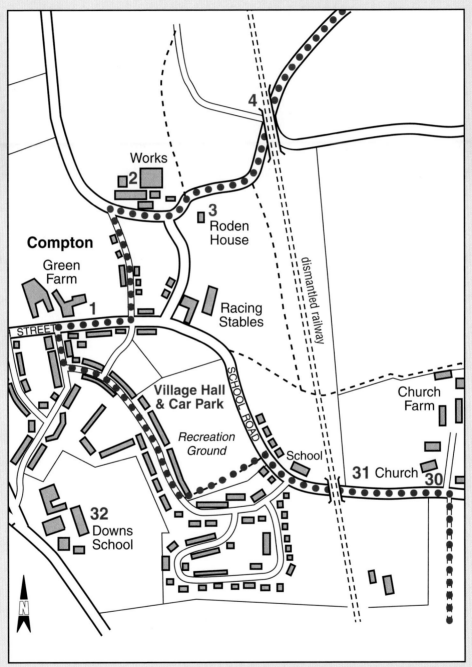

Works

2

Compton

Green
Farm

3
Roden
House

1

Racing
Stables

STREET

dismantled railway

Village Hall
& Car Park

SCHOOL ROAD

*Recreation
Ground*

School

Church
Farm

32
Downs
School

31 Church 30

N

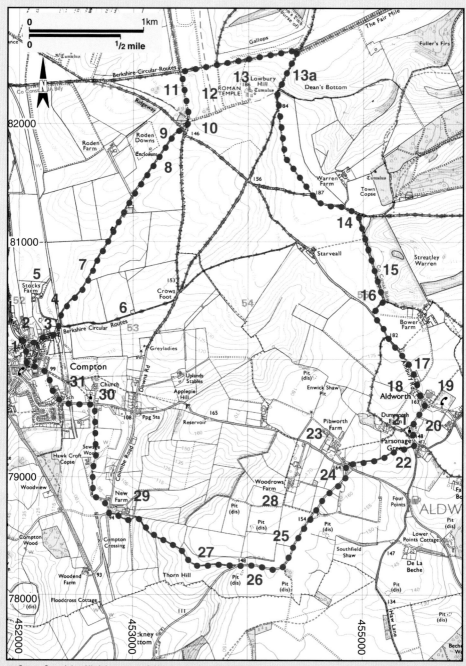

6. The Windmill. This was a post mill and was brought from Little Hungerford, near Hermitage, about 1760.

7. Hedges. The 1761 map shows these tracks passing through enclosed fields. The modern hedges are species poor.

8. Chalkland Flora. Because the tracks were formed while the Downs were open grazing they were spared the ploughing and spraying of post-WW2 agriculture and are rich in chalkland plants. In their season, look for white violets, cowslips, mugwort, knapweed, mint, yarrow, birds foot trefoil, sweet agrimony, scabious, silverweed, red bartsia, toadflax, poppies, harebells, ladies bedstraw, wild carrot, wild parsnip, campanula, mullein and plantain. Pasque flower was once to be seen near Lowbury.

The Compton post mill c1900
With acknowledgements to Mrs M Jarret

9. Roden Down. A Roman enclosure and burial site was excavated here in 1946 finding 1st/2nd Century cremations and 4th/5th century burials.

10. Butterflies. The result of the rich vegetation is a similar richness of butterflies, moths and insects.

11. Birds. Look for rooks, partridges, buzzards and red kites. Listen for larks and peewits.

12. Grassland and gallops. This area is particularly flower rich, especially with cowslips. The regular mowing of the gallops has mimicked sheep grazing and preserved the flora. In spring this particular gallop is a yellow band of cowslips.The racing industry's move to all weather tracks is threatening the survival of these gallops. Excellent views over the down land and to the south.

13. Lowbury Hill. [This field is private]. This is the site of a Roman enclosure with religious significance and a Saxon burial mound. *Low* means burial mound and *bury* probably refers to the remains of the enclosure. The site was excavated in 1913-14 and re-excavated in 1994. The temple was in use from about 200AD to 400AD. In the barrow a Saxon aristocrat aged about 60 was buried with his sword and spear in about 620AD. The low bank now visible is not ancient – it was built after the 1913-14 excavation. The views include Wittenham Clumps, Beacon Hill and the Chiltern scarp.

The triangulation pillar is now obsolete and is maintained as a memorial to a surveying instructor.

13A. Ancient road. Contrast this deeply sunk old track with the path at Point 14. Note, especially in early summer, the richness of the flora on the banks. Look for lady's bedstraw, hedge bedstraw, strawberries, salad burnet, knapweed, self heal, black medic, agrimony, St John's wort, scabious, heartsease and many others.

Streatley Warren 1975

14. Species poor hedges. These also may result from 18th-19th century enclosures. They are mainly blackthorn and hawthorn with some field maple, wayfaring tree, elder and briar.

15. Streatley Warren. This is a 'Celtic Field System'. Excavations show that the banks date from the Iron Age and the fields were in use in the Roman period. It is a SSSI for chalk grassland. Under the Countryside & Rights of Way Act 2000 which came into force in 2005 it has become open to access. The owner may close it during the lambing season and during the nesting season for ground nesting birds. The 'warren' name indicates that it was used to rear rabbits in the medieval period when their meat and fur were valuable.

16. Pre-enclosure roads. Note the large lynchet along the western side. The deep cutting was caused by centuries of wear.

17. Sunken road. Note again how deeply centuries of wear have cut this road into the landscape.

18. Chapel (1861). The area was strongly Methodist in the 19th century. There were many more chapels than churches. Most of them are now disused or converted to houses. The former Village School is attached to the chapel.

19. The Bell. This famous pub has been in the landlord's family for several generations. The house is a five bay cruck open hall carbon 14 dated to 1340. Note the Fire Mark under the eaves showing that the Phoenix insurance company was providing cover for the building.

20. The Well. This was dug in 1868 and is 370 feet deep (113 metres) and about 328 feet (100 metres) to the water surface. It has been filled and capped. Before the well was dug water would have been collected from roofs and stored in underground cisterns. Waterborne disease was common. In very dry weather water for stock was collected in water wagons from the pond at Burnt Hill.

Compton The Bell Aldworth

The Phoenix firemark

21. Church. The lower half of the tower is dated to about 1200 and the church is famous for the de la Beche effigies (Aldworth giants). Their castle was on the site of De la Beche Manor with a deer park (1335) to the south. They were a powerful and influential family. One was tutor to the Black Prince in c.1340. The font is Norman. An ancient yew in the churchyard may be as old as, or older than, the church. The vegetation in the churchyard is managed under 'The Living Churchyard & Cemetery Project'.

22. Oak. Look for the 5 foot (1.5m) diameter pollard oak which may be 400 years old.

The well at Aldworth

23. Pibworth Farm. Emily Selwood, the wife of Alfred Tennyson, the famous Victorian poet lived here.

24. Potash pit & saw pit. The small round pit may have been for making potash and the long narrow pit opposite is probably a back-filled saw pit.

25. Woodland relic hedge and badger sett. Note the dense bluebells along this hedge and the massive lime and beech stools. This hedge is a strip of retained ancient woodland.

26. Species Rich Hedge. Look for dogwood, field maple, hazel, blackthorn, spindle, briar.

Aldworth church yew tree.

27. Ancient boundary. There is a huge lynchet to the north formed as ploughing moved soil down hill over centuries. The bank is one long rabbit warren. In season look for :- spindle, blackthorn, hawthorn, field maple, elder, dogwood. marjoram, yarrow, sweet agrimony, campion, scabious, perforate St John's Wort.

Aldworth Church

28. Woodrows Farm. Reputed to be visited by a ghostly carriage and horses. 4th century Roman pottery kilns were found in the field to the west. One was lifted intact and is now in store at the Science Museum in London.

29. New Farm. Was probably 'new' at least 400 years ago. The present house seems to be early 19th century, but the barn is much older. Note the granary on staddle stones to prevent rats climbing in to eat the seed.

30. Compton church. The font is mid 12th century and the lower tower is probably 13th century. It was heightened in 1614. The whole church was re-modelled in 1850. It has a brass of about 1500 and an early record chest. A splendid embroidered parish map was made for The Millennium and hangs in the church. Note the mounting block by the gate and the cast iron grave markers. The large Victorian house south of the road was originally the Rectory.

31. Deserted Medieval Village. The humps and bumps in the field to the west of the church are the remains of part of the medieval village. It may have been cleared to make a park for Roden House.

32. The Downs School. Was founded as a Secondary Modern School in 1960 for those children who did not pass the 11+ exam to go to a grammar school. It became the smallest Comprehensive School in the country in 1973. It has developed into a large and respected school with a Sixth Form and it specialises in teaching languages.

Sources and further reading

Victoria County History – Berkshire

Morris J (Ed)	*Domesday Book – Berkshire* Phillimore 1979
Wood M	*Domesday – a search for the roots of England* BBC 1986
Ekwall E (ed)	*The Concise Dictionary of English Place-names* OUP 1974
McMahon L & Mankin D	*The Story of Compton – A Berkshire Downland & Village* Compton Parish Council 2000
Fulford M & Rippon S et al	*Lowbury Hill, Oxon: a re-assessment of the probable Romano-Celtic temple and the Anglo-Saxon barrow.* Archaelogical Journal 1994
Mr Macauley	*History of The Bell* personal communication 2004
Mabey R	*Flora Britannica* Chatto & Windus 1997

CHAPTER THREE

Chasing the White Hart
Ashampstead and Hampstead Norreys

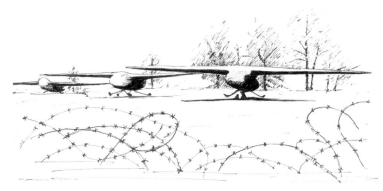

Ashampstead is not mentioned as such in Domesday Book. However, the site had probably already been settled as an outlying hamlet of the manor of Basildon and used to exploit the local arable land and woodland. It was probably called *Assedone*, which means *valley where ash trees grow*. Assedone has not been positively located, but the Domesday acreage for Assedone is about right for Ashampstead and the tenant family in 1086 is known in later documents to have held land in the area.

By this date it is clear that the land was already mainly open arable land with dispersed settlements working their neighbouring fields and woods, a pattern that has hardly changed to the present day.

There are many small flower-rich ancient woods and coppices. These are surrounded by large banks and ditches on which grow massive coppice stools. The enclosure was probably carried out in the 13th century when landowners realised that the vital woodland resource was being destroyed by agriculture.

As well as intensively managed coppices there were two deer parks. The park at Ashampstead Common seems to have been built about 1240 by the lord of the manor of Bradfield while the one in Beche Park Wood was built under licence by the de la Beche family of Aldworth in 1335. The boundary bank of the de la Beche park cut off the medieval road from Haw Farm to Aldworth and diverted it around the western side of the park causing the dangerous double bend in the B4009. At the eastern end of the boundary the steep valley side was used instead of a bank and the Bradfield to Aldworth road was diverted away from the easy gradient of the valley bottom, up a short steep hill and along a terrace to rejoin the old route at Grim's Ditch. Thus one family's arrogance caused inconvenience to their neighbours for nearly 800 years!

Haw Farm Airfield was a satellite airfield for the main airfield at Harwell. Building started in 1938 and it was commissioned in 1940. In the process two small farms called Buttonshaw Farm and Turville Farm were demolished.

A Douglas Havoc at How Farm in WW2

The airfield was used mainly for the training of Wellington bomber crews and as a base for ferrying hundreds of Wellingtons to the Middle East via Gibraltar and Malta. Later in the war it was used to train the pilots of troop carrying gliders. It was bombed on three occasions. After the war it was used by the Fleet Air Arm. It was then decommissioned and returned to agriculture, but many war time relics remain. For example, the narrow strip of trees marks a runway and there are several pill boxes, air raid shelters and a munitions store.

There are many stories about the airfield. After one raid returning bombers were diverted here because their own field was under attack. Several ran off the end of the runway into the field beyond the road and one sat on the road with a collapsed undercarriage. When it was lifted a crushed van was found beneath it, the driver of which was still alive! The other aircraft were towed back from the field along the road and the roadside lime trees were still small enough for a gang of men to bend them down so that the wings could pass over them!

The area still has a strong connection with flying. It is a Registered Airfield and is still used by light aircraft. The strange structure on the west side is a Doppler VHF Omni-Range radio beacon marking the centre line of the outward bound airway from Heathrow.

Airway beacon

Hampstead Norreys Manor Farm and Church 1969.

With acknowledgemments to Mr & Mrs R Betts.

Hampstead Norreys is a much older settlement than Ashampstead. See Chapter 5. The name *hamstead* means *farm settlement* in Early English. The church has Saxon elements and the positioning of an early church immediately next to the manor house probably indicates that village was the administrative centre of a large estate. Domesday Book tells us that it had belonged to King Edward before the Norman Conquest. The estate probably extended north and south along the valley and up onto the hills on either side. There were smaller settlements exploiting local resources at Eling and Wyld Court in the same way that Ashampstead was used by the estate centred on Lower Basildon. The parish developed out of the estate and originally extended as far south as Hermitage.

In 1086 the manor was held by Theodoric the Goldsmith. In the 12th century the village was called *Hampstead Sifrewast.* This changed to *Hampstead Norreys* in 1450 when the manor was bought by the Norreys family of Bray.

Much of the arable land was farmed as Open Fields in which tenants (properly called *husbandmen*) held a number of acre or half-acre strips of land scattered around the fields. They were based in small farmsteads in the villages rather than in farms on their holdings. In the earliest times they held the land by working for set periods of time on the land of the lord of the manor and they were bound to the manor and could not leave without the lord's permission. In later periods these *services* were commuted for cash rents.

The Open Fields were enclosed by Act of Parliament in 1773 and 1778 and produced the landscape we now see around us.

Many of the woods are very ancient. This is indicated not only by their rich flora but also by the well preserved archaeological features within them.

This walk includes Ashampstead village, Haw Farm and Hampstead Norreys village. It starts and finishes at Ashampstead.

- It is about 6 miles or 9 km long. The route is along wide, clear and well marked tracks.
- There is a very steep hill and surfaces can be uneven and muddy.
- The route crosses the busy B4009 and agricultural machinery and vehicles use some of the tracks on the old airfield.
- Light aircraft taking off, landing and taxi-ing may be encountered on the airfield.
- Look out for horses and riders.

Ordnance Survey map Explorer 158 'Newbury and Hungerford' will be useful.

1. Ashampstead School was built in 1873-75 on land granted by the Hopkins Estate of Tidmarsh. It was funded by public subscription and served as the local school until December 1971. It was bought by the village for use as the Village Hall. Great resentment was caused when the Church Commissioners demanded the full market value, even though the Church had contributed little to its founding.

2. The church was built in the late 12th century and was originally a chapel subordinate to the church at Lower Basildon. Ashampstead was originally part of the manor, and later the parish, of Basildon and chapels were built in large parishes to save church goers a long walk. The yew stump in the wall is traditionally the remains of the tree under which the first services were held. There is also a legend that plague victims were buried on this side of the church. The yew on the south side was planted about 1700.

Ashampstead church

Yew tree in north wall

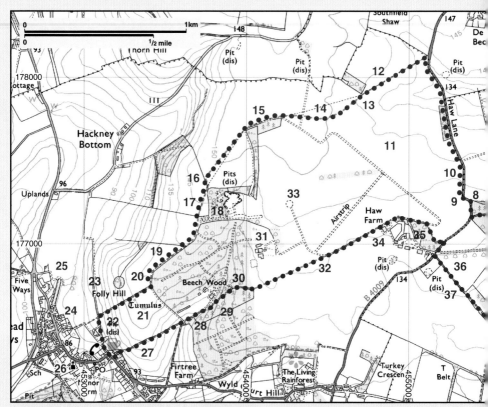

3. Holly Lane was the original track from the Bottom Road, (the old north-south route) via Ashampstead Green to Haw Farm and Hampstead Norreys. The four long shallow depressions scattered beside the track are partially filled saw pits.

4. Ashampstead Green was the village playing field until the first Lord Iliffe granted Flowers Piece to the village as a Recreation Ground.

5. Old road. Note the substantial bank on each side. This track led to the village from the fields that preceded Beche Park Wood. It then continued to the south down Pinfold Lane. The small huts in the field are pheasant rearing arks.

6. Ancient Woodland. The rich ground flora shows that these woods have been here a very long time. In spring, look for: dense bluebells, wood anemone, wood spurge, wood sorrel, yellow archangel, dog's mercury and many others.

7. Bundle planted beech. This interesting tree is actually more than one tree. It is the result of a number of seedlings being planted together or as a result of several beech nuts in a squirrel's hoard germinating and growing successfully.

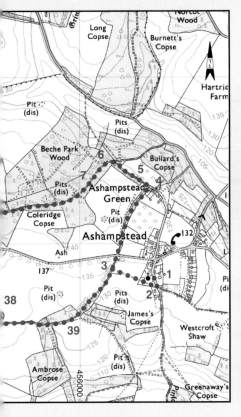

Bundle planted beech

8. The de la Beche Deer Park. The long curving bank, built soon after 1336 as the park pale of a deer park, forced the medieval road from Haw farm to Aldworth to divert, causing this awkward bend. A similar diversion on the east side forced the Bottom Road up a short steep hill that must have been a nuisance to every laden cart for 600 years!

9. Permitted Path. Yattendon Estate have agreed with West Berkshire Council to create a path along the field edge linking the footpath at Haw Farm to the east-west cross field path further north.

The de la Beche Park
Pale highlighted with bluebells

This is a legal Permitted Path, not a Public Right of Way and can be revoked after a stipulated notice period. The wide field margin was created as part of the Stewardship Plan. These wide margins are very valuable for wildlife.

A local defence pill box

10. Species rich hedge. Species rich hedges tend to be older than species poor hedges. Look for: field maple, blackthorn, hawthorn, hazel, elm, ash, briar and beech.

11. Open Fields. In 1972 these fields were transferred from Ashampstead parish to Hampstead Norreys. They were originally the Common Fields of the sub-manor of Coleridge. Coleridge means *the ridge of the charcoal burners.*

12. Pill box. The airfield was surrounded by these small forts. An invading army must capture airfields as soon as possible in order to bring in supplies and troops. Defenders armed with light machine guns manned these pill boxes to protect the airfield.

13. Buttonshaw. A small farm on this site was demolished to make room for the airfield.

14. Chalk pit. These shallow hollows are partially filled pits from which chalk was dug to spread on the surrounding field. The soils covering the chalk rock are often very acid and their pH must be raised if cereals are to thrive.

15. Wood edge. There is a splendid view across the upper Pang Valley from this point. It ranges from the cone of Oareborough Hill to the south to the radio mast above Wantage to the north. Look also for buzzards, red kites and roe deer. There are some very large coppice stools of sycamore and field maple on the wood bank.

16. Human and badger boundary. Look for the scatter of badger dung pits as you pass through the hedge. Badgers use their latrines to mark the edge of their territory.

17. Bird seed. This corner contains a mixture of kale and quinoa planted as part of the farm Stewardship Plan to provide winter food for wild birds and pheasants.

18. Bomb store. This wood is private and permission must be obtained from

A wartime munitions store being taken over by nature

Yattendon Estate to visit it. Munitions were stored here, well away from the airfield, so that minimum damage would be caused by an explosion. The banks would direct the blast upwards. Note the badger sett in the bank.

19. Wood bank. Note the large bank just inside the wood. The massive ancient coppice stools show that the bank itself is very old. In spring the bank is covered in bluebells and other ancient woodland plants.

20. View point. A splendid view across the valley and down over the village. Look for buzzards.

21. Burial mound. Now ploughed away, it was probably a Bronze Age round barrow dating from about 2500BC. A very slight hump is still just detectable, especially just after the field has been drilled.

22. Species rich hedge. The replanting and gapping up of this hedge was one of the first tasks undertaken by the Pang Valley Conservation Volunteers.

23. Old road. This track is part of the ancient route up the Pang Valley from the south to the Ridgeway in the north.

24. Cricket field. Before the village was given the Dean Meadow this was the cricket field.

25. River Pang. The Pang is a *bourne* which means a stream which regularly dries up. It is fed from ground-water springs in the chalk and these need wet winters to recharge them. The perennial head is at the Blue Pools below Stanford Dingley.

26. The village is described in the main note section.

27. Species rich hedge and lynchet. This hedge is growing on an ancient boundary. Ploughing has loosened the soil which has then moved down hill. It has collected on the uphill side of the hedge and moved away on the downhill side to form a step or lynchet. Look for: blackthorn, hazel, wayfaring tree, briar, spindle, elder, hawthorn, dogwood and a walnut tree.

28. Holloway. This narrow trench has been worn by generations of feet. Probably many of them were those of RAF personnel coming back from the pubs in Hampstead Norreys!

29. Beech Wood. Part way up the hill the path crosses a bank and the ground vegetation changes. In spring you will see the change more clearly since the up hill area is covered in bluebells. This probably indicates that the area below the cross bank is an old hazel coppice planted in a previously cultivated field, whereas the area above the bank is an ancient wood. Note the large amount of standing and fallen deadwood which provides very valuable habitats for many creatures.

Air raid shelter

30. Air raid shelter. This was one of many that served the workshops and training blocks that once stood on the edge of the wood.

Grain dryer

31. Pig unit. Once a 'state of the art' unit, it was built in 1972 to house 220 breeding sows and their offspring. Following the devastating slump in pig prices in the 1990s it was leased to a specialist pig producing company but they too were unable to make it pay and the unit is now closed.

32. Beetle bank. This strip of rough grass is retained to house insect predators which move out into the crops and prey on insect pests. It is an effective way of reducing pesticide use.

33. Airway beacon. As explained in the general notes, this strange structure marks the centreline of the airliner corridor out of Heathrow.

34. Grain dryer. Built in 2000, this computer controlled unit dries 48 tonnes of grain an hour. It can also store 8,000 tonnes of grain.

35. Haw Farm is a very ancient site. The name means *enclosures* in Early English and it appears on the earliest maps. I suspect that in early times the area was a cattle and sheep rearing area. Several green lanes lead away from it down which animals were driven to market.

36. Lime trees. The road side lime trees are those mentioned in the general notes as being bent over when the bombers were recovered.

37. Dog Lane was Ashampstead's link to the west before the modern road was built in the 1930s. In the early morning and late afternoon village children walked along it and then down the road to Hampstead Norreys station to catch the train to Newbury to attend the grammar schools in the town.

38. Pig unit. This unit suffered the same fate as the Haw Farm unit.

39. Re-used dairy. The former dairy unit on this site was made redundant by the large dairy unit at Frilsham Home Farm. Yattendon Estate has a policy of re-using redundant sites and it has been put to good use by an international game dealer. Lorries arrive here from many European countries and go away loaded with deer, pheasants and wild boar. It has a retail unit which sells many interesting meat products. Look out for wild boar in the pens.

Sources and further reading

Victoria County History – Berkshire

Morris J (Ed)	*Domesday Book – Berkshire* Phillimore 1979	
Wood M	*Domesday – a search for the roots of England* BBC 1986	
Ekwall E (ed)	*The Concise Dictionary of English Place-names* OUP 1974	
Williamson T	*Shaping Medieval Landscapes* Windgather Press 2003	
Mabey R	*Flora Britannica* Chatto & Windus 1997	
Bowyer MJF	*Action Stations! 6. Military airfields of the Cotswolds and central Midlands* Stevens, Cambridge 1983	

CHAPTER FOUR

Walk in an ancient landscape
Ashampstead Parish

The Open Fields. There are many theories about the origin of Open Field agriculture, but it is certainly a very ancient practice. In England it is now only followed at Laxton and in Wales on the Gower Peninsula. The system was very complex and had many local variations, but in essence large un-hedged fields were subdivided into blocks about 220 yards (c.201m) long called *furlongs.* These in their turn were subdivided into *strips* about 22 yards (20m) wide, each containing an acre of land. An acre was defined as the amount of land that could be ploughed by an ox team in a day and a furlong (furrow long) was as far as they could go without a rest. *Husbandmen* lived together in villages or scattered hamlets and held a number of strips scattered across the various furlongs. This gave everyone a fair share of the good and poor land. The *Manor Court* decided which crop would be grown on a given furlong and everyone grew the same. Initially rents were paid in services to the *Lord of the Manor.* These could be ploughing and harvesting on the Lord's strips or carrying messages etc. Later cash rents were paid. This was a very inefficient system and the amalgamation of strips into enclosed fields took place from at least the 13th century. The last survivors were enclosed by Act of Parliament in the 19th & 20th centuries. The system has left its marks; curving, S shaped hedges with very little ground flora in the hedge bottom are usually enclosed strips and a cricket pitch at 22 yards, is the length of a ploughman's setting out chain!

The Coppice Cycle. Managing woods to produce crops of standard size sticks and poles at short intervals goes back to the Neolithic Period – at least 6,000 years ago. However, the widespread conversion of *wood pasture* (low density woods in which animals grazed) to *coppices* seems to have started in the 12th and 13th centuries as the population grew and so much land was cleared for arable farming that wood supplies became threatened. *Coppicing* involves cutting a deciduous tree near ground level and allowing it to shoot. The shoots are then cut at short intervals (1, 8, 15 years etc) to supply poles of the size required. Nearly all deciduous trees will coppice, but the most usual in this area are hazel, alder and ash followed by maple, beech and oak. In other areas hornbeam and sweet chestnut were coppiced. Dedicating an area of an ancient wood pasture as coppice preserved the flora growing in the wood. Ancient coppices are flower rich. The years of shade after the canopy closed suppressed coarse herbage such as bramble and bracken which would have suppressed the more delicate plants. The burst of light after felling allowed the flowers to flourish and spread. Most of our best bluebell woods are ancient coppices.

Ancient Woodland Indicator Species. A wood known to have existed in 1600 is classed as *Ancient Secondary Woodland.* We have no primary woodland in Britain, except possibly on some inaccessible gorge sides, but many woods are over a thousand years old. Hawkridge Wood (Frilsham) was there to be granted to Abingdon Abbey in 956AD to supply oaks to rebuild their church.

These woods have rich ground floras, particularly of plants which have poor seed dispersal mechanisms. Plants such as burdock have prickly seeds with covers which attach themselves to animals' coats and to human clothing allowing the seeds to be transported long distances. Other plants such as

dandelions have light seeds equipped with sails that are carried by the wind. But plants such as wood anemones spread slowly by rhizomes and much of their seed is sterile and does not persist long in the seed bank; once destroyed they are unlikely to return. Their presence thus indicates that the ground has been undisturbed for a long time. Ancient Woodland Indicator Plants are plants such as bluebell, wood anemone, yellow archangel,

Wood anemone & bluebells

Spurge laurel

Wood sorrel

Primrose

Early purple orchid

dog's mercury, primrose, sweet woodruff, early purple orchid, spurge laurel, wood sorrel, ramsons, Solomon's seal etc. The more listed plants a wood has, the better the chance of it being ancient.

Natural England provides a list of those plants which can be used to identify Ancient Woods and local Ecological Record Centres are working on local lists. A copy of the list can be obtained from *Natural England*.

The Black Death. In the winter of 1348–9 Britain, along with much of Europe, was stuck by a devastating epidemic. It was known as the Black Death. Anyone contracting it was dead within a few days. It was thought to have been bubonic plague transmitted by fleas carried by the black rat. This is now believed to be unlikely and that it was more probably a viral infection akin to the influenza epidemic which struck northern Europe in the years after the First World war.

Very large numbers of people were killed. Some communities were wiped out, others suffered 50% losses. The manor records for the Manor of Basildon state that no rents were paid that year since all the tenants were dead. It is impossible to imagine the horror of such an experience. The disease returned on numerous occasions in the subsequent years and suppressed population growth until the 17th century.

The population had been growing steadily since the 9th century but agricultural technology had not grown with it. To feed the people farmers had been forced on to marginal land. In some places they pushed their ploughs along the sides of steep hill slopes and in doing so created plough terraces. The collapse of the population allowed these to be abandoned and many are concealed in our woods.

Solomons seal & bluebells   *Ramsons & bluebells*

This walk includes Childs Court Farm, Ashampstead Parish and Ashampstead Common. It starts and finishes at Childs Court.

- It is about 6 miles or 9½ km long. The route is along wide, clear and well marked tracks.
- There are three modest hills and surfaces can be uneven and muddy.
- There are a number of road crossings and some short lengths of road walking.
- Horses and riders may be encountered.

Ordnance Survey map Explorer 159 Reading will be useful.

Geology. Although chalk occurs at depth, it is often covered by later sediments. These are dominated by clay but there are also some areas of sand and gravel. These materials are the parents of the acid Berkhamstead, Winchester and Swanmore Series soils. There are some areas of the more calcareous Coombe Series soils where the chalk is close to the surface or in dry valleys where eroded chalk has collected. These soils are pervious so there are almost no springs or streams.

1. Child's Court Farm. This was a purpose built farm complex established about 1680 when the fields around it were converted from Open Fields to Enclosed Fields. Note the two barns and the farm house neatly grouped around a yard. The sizes of the barns reflect the relative importance of the crops they held. The larger eastern barn was the Wheat Barn and the smaller western barn was the Barley Barn. Wheat bread was the 'staff of life' whilst barley was mainly made into malt for beer brewing.

Childs Court Farm about 1930

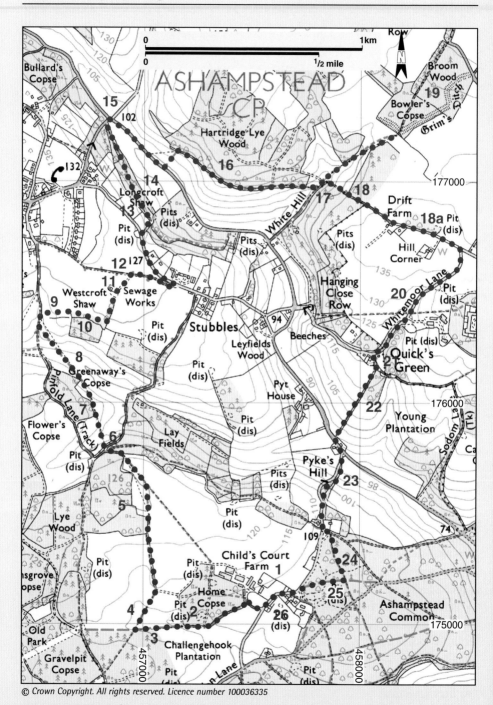

2. Home Copse. This copse supplied the farm with the vast numbers of poles and sticks needed in the pre-plastic era and with firewood, before the introduction of railways in the early 19C made cheap coal available.

3. Species rich hedge. These bushes line the ancient road from Ashampstead Common to Hampstead Norreys via Wyld Court. It contains *berberis* which was valued as a hedging plant because of its vicious spines. In the 19C it was identified as a host for rust in wheat and was almost eradicated.

4. The Avenue. This field was first recorded in 1355 when it was known as *Cockenhead Down.* Later this became *Coxey Down.* The Xmas Trees were planted in 2001 and will be harvested between 2008 and 2010. The seed comes from Georgia. The seedlings are produced in France and Denmark and planted out at 3 years old.

Dr Breach 1906

5. Doctor's Copse. Named for Dr Breach of Yattendon who bought it in 1908. It consists of two ancient bluebell-rich coppices with an old field between them. The large ash stools on the boundary banks are between 400 and 1000 years old and indicate the antiquity of the banks.

6. Leyfields Meadow. This is an important piece of unimproved grassland. It has been wooded and open more than once in its history and this is reflected in its rich flora. It is a County Wildlife Heritage Site and the Pang Valley Conservation Volunteers assist the owners with its management.

7. Greenaway's Copse. The flora demonstrates the value of plants as indicators of historic land use. The southern part is an ancient bluebell copse but the northern extension was added in the 19thC and has a dense mat of dog's mercury.

8. South Field. This was one of the original Open Fields of the settlement. It had already been enclosed by the time of the first detailed map in 1845.

9. Species rich hedge. This hedge separates South Field from Church Field (another Open Field). The 13 hardwood species and many woodland plants in the hedge bottom show that this is a relic of the original woods which covered the area. Look for spindle, field maple, dogwood, crab, wayfaring tree and others plus bluebell, yellow archangel, primrose.

10. Badger sett. This very large sett is ancient and still active. Beware of holes! Badgers live mainly on earthworms which they gather from grassland when the worms surface at night – hence the texture of the dung! A dry spring and a dry summer cause severe mortality amongst badger cubs. Badgers are clean animals. Note the latrine pits away from the sett which are also used as territory markers.

11. Chalk quarry. Chalk was used to raise the pH of the acid soils to allow wheat to be grown. As much as 80 cubic feet was ploughed into an acre.

12. The Chalk Path & Crydress. The path is shown on maps of 1761. The field is another of the early Open Fields. It may once have been a coppice since its name comes from the Early English word *hress* which means *underwood*. The overgrown hedge behind the houses is another woodland relic and still contains bluebells.

13. Long Croft. These long narrow fields were held as private land by early farmers. Sometimes they were cultivated but often they held the plough oxen and horses. The hedges are woodland relics.

14. Longcroft Shaw. The population of the country increased rapidly between c.900 and 1300AD but farming technology did not keep pace. Cereal yields were often as low as 3 or 4 times the seed sown. Modern yields can be x60. Farmers were forced to use marginal land such as this steep hillside. A severe climatic downturn in c.1300 caused famine. The Black Death followed in 1348-9 and returned at intervals thereafter. The population was cut by half or more. In the Manor of Basildon all the tenants were reported as dead. The marginal land was abandoned and reverted to grass or wood but the ploughing had caused the terraces, *lynchets*, along the slope. Look for, in season: sweet woodruff, wood anemone, bluebell, dog's mercury .... Look also for the two shallow rectangular pits beside the path. These are back-filled sawpits.

Sweet woodruff

15. Bottom Road. This ordinary looking country road is very ancient. It is a natural route from the south along the bottom of a dry valley, where the gradients are slight, to the Ridgeway in the north. It is lined

Dog's mercury

with large lynchets where ploughing has loosened soil which has then moved down hill and collected against the road boundary to make a positive lynchet. Where the soil has moved down hill away from the road it has created a negative lynchet. These are particularly noticeable where we cross the road later at Pyt House. Part of the Norman army probably marched along it in 1066 after camping at Englefield on their way to cross the Thames at Wallingford and then on to attack London from the north. They may even have camped in the valley in front of us. The evidence for this is the trail of devastation the army left in its wake shown by the fall in manor values in Domesday Book. Both Hartridge and 'Ashden' (Ashampstead) fell by 50%. The road is also the most practical route for an army moving from Winchester to Wallingford. The road from Pangbourne along the Thames is on a narrow terrace with the river on one side and an extremely steep hill on the other where the army would have no room to manoeuvre if attacked

16. Hartridge Lye Wood. This wood has a rich flora but it also contains ancient fields. Domesday Book records Hartridge Manor as having only enough woodland to graze 3 pigs, but the inspectors may not have included areas of coppice. In 1309 there were about 13 acres and in 1466 about 46 acres. The 14C cold period and the population crash caused much arable land to be converted to grazing and coppice. Along the wood edge look for, in season: wood spurge, primroses, violets, roast beef plant (stinking iris – once used as a purgative), spurge laurel (not a spurge nor a laurel but a daphne – poisonous), bluebells, cowslips... There are also the remains of an ancient beech hedge, some important standing deadwood and badger setts. Buzzards and red kites are often seen around this wood.

17. Drift Lane. This was an access route to Basildon Common (now Upper Basildon) from Hartridge. The element *drift* means *drove* road.

18. Lime kiln & chalk quarry. This pit was used for making small quantities of lime by burning chalk dug from the quarry which lies just beyond it. These small kilns are known as *farmers' kilns* and the lime was used to make mortar for building and whitewash for painting. A magnetometer survey in 2006 showed that the ground had been subjected to intense heating. The quantities that could be made in a pit of this size would have been insignificant for agricultural purposes. Raw chalk was used to sweeten the land until the improvements in transport enabled mass produced lime made in purpose built kilns to be distributed cheaply and easily. There is another lime kiln and quarry combination further along Drift Lane.

19. Grim's Dyke. This large earthwork is probably 2000 years old but there is no evidence for its date or function. It stands in isolation and may never

An abandoned plough terrace

have been completed. Saxon settlers credited anything they thought beyond the work of human hands to their gods and *Grim* was a by-name for *Woden* or *Odin*. This monument is on private land and permission should be obtained to explore it.

20. Ancient lane. This lane runs along a plough terrace. The humps in the road are the headlands at either end of the strip where the plough was turned.

21. Quick's Green. These small *Greens* are often found around the edges of commons. Squatters settled on unvisited pieces of waste and would be fined annually by the Manor Court. Eventually the fine became a rent.

This area was fervently Methodist in the 19C and the Chapel was built by Isaac Nullis, the son of Ashampstead's grocer and a noted preacher. The lane leading to it is called *Sodom Lane!*

22. Brian's Path. The species rich hedges should indicate ancient origins, but hedge-daters beware! Photographs show that there was nothing here in

Quicks Green chapel c 1890

1930. This path is named for a local resident, Brian Woodage, who has cared for it for many years.

23. Pykes Hill. Named for Pykes Farm which stood at the bottom of the hill. Look for dung pits marking a badger boundary as you enter the path

24. Ashampstead Common. This is an area of ancient wood pasture. It was a deer park from the early 13C. It is very species rich in trees and ground flora and in exotic trees planted by the 19C landowner. It is a County Wildlife Heritage Site and is being sensitively managed by Yattendon Estates under a Twenty Year Forestry Management Scheme. An earlier management plan was developed under which the owners, the Parish Council, local people and the Pang Valley Conservation Volunteers co-operate to look after this fascinating woodland.

25. Old Road. This was the original road to the farm avoiding steep hills. Finding routes without steep gradients is important for a horse with a laden cart.

26. Early House. This house was built in the 14C as an Open Hall. The main room was open to the roof and had a fire in the middle on the floor.

Sources and further reading

Victoria County History – Berkshire

Morris J (Ed)	*Domesday Book – Berkshire* Phillimore 1979	
Wood M	*Domesday – a search for the roots of England* BBC 1986	
Ekwall E (ed)	*The Concise Dictionary of English Place-names* OUP 1974	
Mabey R	*Flora Britannica* Chatto & Windus 1997	
Williamson T	*Shaping Medieval Landscapes* Windgather Press 2003	
Greenaway D & Ward D (eds)	*In the Valley of the Pang* 2002	
Brooks, JE.,	*The Deserted Medieval Villages of North Berkshire* (Unpublished Ph.D. thesis). University of Reading	
Natural England	*Ancient Woodland Vascular Plants* www.naturalengland.org.uk/publications	

CHAPTER FIVE

Historic Hampstead
Exploring the southern part of
Hampstead Norreys parish

Hampstead Norreys
'Motte' or barrow.

Hampstead Norreys. The name means *'farm place'* and there has been a settlement of some kind here for at least a thousand years. There may well have been people living here for as much as three thousand years since there are Bronze Age burial mounds close to the north and south of the village.

The manor is listed in Domesday Book as having belonged to King Edward the Confessor. William the Conqueror claimed that Edward had willed the throne to him and that Harold was a usurper. After the Conquest the manor had been allocated to Theodoric the Goldsmith. The name changed to *Hampstead Sifrewast* in the 12th century and to *Hampstead Norreys* when the manor was bought by the Norreys family of Bray in 1450.

Bronze Age Barrows. Over the dozen millennia that people have lived in this valley they have chosen many different ways to dispose of their dead. You may remember the Neolithic long barrow above East Ilsley discussed in Chapter One. In the Bronze Age one ritual involved interment under mounds of earth. These mounds were generally circular and are known to us as *barrows.* Over the four millennia since their creation many of them have been ploughed flat. We saw an example of this in Chapter Three. However, a very fine surviving example exists in Park Wood where it was protected from ploughing by the creation of a deer park some time before 1551. It has been interpreted rather romantically as a Norman motte. Mottes were mounds within Norman fortifications.

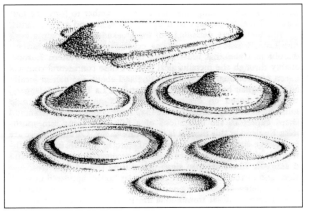

British barrow types long bowl bell disc saucer pond.
With acknowledgements to James Dyer

They had a stockade on the top and were the defence of last resort. The top of Hampstead Norreys motte will hold sixteen people standing packed together. It would have been a very small castle! Also, there is no sign of the outer fortifications usually associated with a *motte and bailey* castle. It seems more probable that it is actually a barrow and three and a half thousand years older than any motte.

Early Saxon Estates. In the late 9th century AD England was invaded by Danish armies. The whole of the North East and the Midlands were overrun and Wessex was invaded. They were eventually conquered by King Alfred and his descendants, including his daughter, and forced to settle in the North East. They were allowed to retain their own laws and customs and the area became known as the Danelaw. Even today it is still identifiable by the many place-names of Scandinavian origin. Modern research has shown that much of King Alfred's Wessex was divided up into very large estates controlled by the king's immediate family and senior colleagues. These estates were soon sub-divided and tenanted by lesser lords. The smaller estates were constructed so that they had a mixture of land types. Typically the headquarters would be in a valley surrounded by the arable and dairying land but the estate would spread up the valley sides until it met the land of the estate based in the next valley. This remote land would be used for pasture and for supplying woodland products.

King Alfred encouraged the spread of Christianity and literacy, and local lords began to build churches on their estates. They naturally built them conveniently close to their own dwellings. The church and its staff were

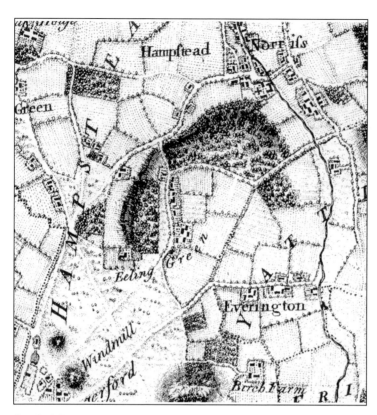

The Eling and Hampstead Norreys area in 1761.

funded by the Tithe. This was a tax in kind amounting to one tenth of the increase of the land; every tenth sheaf, tenth lamb etc. It was levied on the parish and the parish would coincide with the patron's estate. Thus parish boundaries often show us Saxon estates.

Origins of parishes. There was certainly some form of Christian organisation in Southern England in the 4th century. Many early documents refer to British bishops attending synods on the Continent. One papal emissary, Germanus of Auxerre, actually took over a force of local militia in the Chilterns and won a victory over a Saxon war band in 429. He stationed his troops in a steep sided coombe beside the track on which the Saxons were advancing and made them roar *Alleluia!* as the Saxons crossed the valley mouth. The sound was concentrated by the hillside and so shocked and terrified the enemy that they fled without striking a blow.

The Saxon nations were still pagan when they came to Britain and several centuries of missionary work by the Churches of Wales, of Northern Britain, of Ireland and from Rome took place. As ruling elites were converted churches were established at the centres of power. From these mother churches priests went out to minister to the population. They preached in the open at market places or in places already identified as sacred. In the 9th and 10th centuries estate holders began to build churches in their villages and to fund their maintenance from a tax imposed on their own estates. The boundaries of these estates were usually marked by ditches and banks which have sometimes been shown to be very much older than the Saxon Period and may perhaps be the boundaries of Roman or Iron Age land holdings. These features became our parish boundaries and survived intact to the present day

Manor Farm barns, early 20th century
With acknowledgemments to Mr & Mrs R Betts.

Manor farm and church 1969
With acknowledgemments to Mr & Mrs R Betts.

except for minor adjustments and some illogical changes in 1972.

Since the priest's income depended on being able to identify who lived in the parish, he had a vested interest in maintaining the boundary features. Beating the Bounds was an important annual event which took place on Rogation Sunday.

Manor Farm. This is almost certainly on the site of the original Saxon estate headquarters. The Manor House, together with its carefully planned layout of barns and stables, dates from at least the 17th century. As with the typical estate above, its arable land lies to the north of the village in the valley bottom. The Betts family came here in 1909 and their then 9 year old son later married the daughter of the previous farmer who had farmed here from 1817 to 1902. Almost two centuries of care by two families. In the

1920's the farm was famous for pioneering large scale chicken farming.

The modern farm consists of 350 acres of arable land and a 100 head beef herd which rears the bull calves born on Eling Farm. The farm entered the Countryside Steward Scheme and has transferred to the new Entry Level Scheme. This explains the wide field margins and the area behind the White Hart which is sown with wheat, kale and quinoa to provide wild bird food.

Environmental Stewardship. This is a government funded scheme managed by the Department of the Environment, Food and Rural Affairs (defra). It funds farmers and landowners to help them protect existing environmental and historical features and to encourage new habitats for wildlife. This is achieved by putting grass margins around field boundaries to protect existing hedges, by repairing old hedges and planting new, and by recreating wild flower meadows and old grassland in areas where they may have been ploughed out since World War 2. The grassland builds up the population of insects and small mammals and thus supports a larger population of the bird species that feed on them. The margins provide breeding sites for insect predators which spread into the crops and reduce the harmful insect populations. The new hedges provide nest sites and corridors linking other habitats such as woods and copses. In addition to this some farms create public access paths which allow the public to appreciate the countryside and the work of the farming community.

Eling Organic Farm. Eling Farm is rented from The Gerald Palmer Trust by John Goodenough and his son Brian. The family has farmed here since the mid 1920's. Eling Farm covers 1000 acres and other land is rented at Wyld Court, Hermitage and Hamstead Marshall.

In 1998 they took the decision to move to an organic system of farming. This involved a three year change over period before milk could be sold as organic. Today the farm milks on two sites. One at Birch Farm Frilsham, which milks 130 cows calving in the autumn, and one at Eling Farm, which milks 250 cows calving in the spring. At both of these dairies the cows live outside all the year round. For this reason you will see different breeds of cows ranging from British Friesians to Shorthorns. These animals do not give as much milk as conventional dairy cows but they are tougher and live longer and their milk is of better quality.

The key to animal health lies in supplying a balanced and nutritious grass and silage diet. To provide this many different plants are grown in the grass leys on Eling Farm. Red and white clover supply nitrogen to the soil and salad burnet, yarrow and plantains provide minerals. In summer the deep roots of chicory help break up the soil and also deliver minerals.

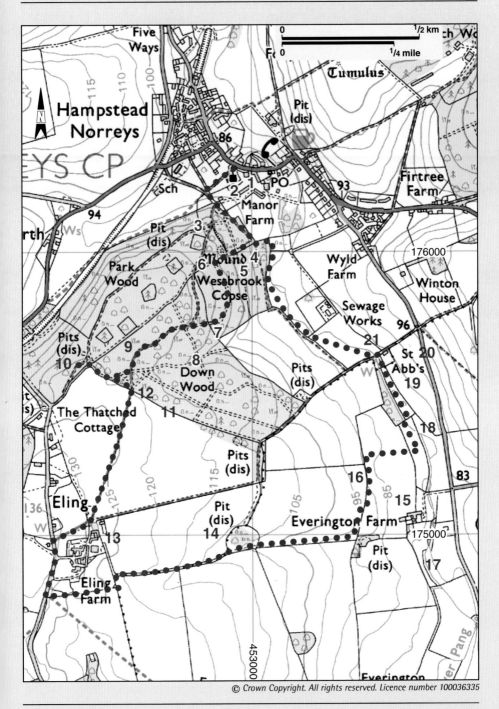

St Mary's church   *The Lousley family cast iron tomb*

This walk includes Hampstead Norreys, Eling Farm and the River Pang
It starts and finishes at Hampstead Norreys Village Hall.

- **It is about 2½ miles or 4 km long. The route is along wide, clear and well marked tracks.**
- **There is a modest hill and surfaces can be uneven and muddy.**
- **Tractors and farm machinery also use the tracks.**
- **Cattle and sheep may be encountered on Eling Farm.**
- **Horses and riders may be met with.**

Ordnance Survey map Explorer 158 'Newbury and Hungerford' will be useful.

1. Manor Farm. The house appears to be 17th century but is certainly built on the site of a sequence of older manor houses probably stretching back to the 9th century.

2. St Mary's church. Built mainly in the early 12th century although some of the fabric may be earlier Saxon work. Both the north and south doors are typically Norman. The nave was re-roofed in 1635 and the church was restored in 1879-80. The pairing of the parish church and the Manor House is typical of late Saxon estate centres. The cast iron tomb of the Lousely family behind the church was made at the Bucklebury foundry from scrap iron collected by friends and admirers of the family.

3. Park Wood. This is Ancient Secondary Woodland and it may have been a medieval deer park. The Lord of the Manor was accused of enclosing 30 acres for parkland in 1515 and this wood is probably the area enclosed. The large boundary bank with the ditch on the inside can be seen snaking

The well   *Hampstead Norreys Motte*

through the trees. The wood is managed by clear-felling blocks of trees and then replanting them with oak, beech, larch, Scot's pine and western hemlock. The many banks and ditches in the wood and its exceptionally rich flora indicate a long and varied history and are the subject of on-going study.

4. Old road. This is one of the old roads from the village up to the commons on the top of the hill. Note the rich flora on the banks showing that they were built in woodland.

5. Westbrook Copse. This wood is planted on old fields, as is shown by the mat of dog's mercury under the trees and the paucity of other flora. Compare its poor flora with the rich flora on the north (right hand) side of the track. That it was an old field is confirmed by 19th century maps.

6. The motte. Mottes are Norman defensive works, usually built soon after the Conquest in 1066. They had a timber stockade around the top and stood within defended yards called *bailies*. As mentioned above, there are doubts as to whether this is a motte. We experimented during a conducted walk and were only able to stand 16 people on the top. A very small castle! Also, there is no sign of a bailey. The mound is more probably a large Bronze Age barrow. **This is a Scheduled Ancient Monument which it is an offence to damage or disturb.**

Guidance: turn sharp left at the path junction about 130m uphill beyond the motte.

7. Sawpit. This is about 20 yards east of the bank which crosses the path. The shallow hollow is the remains of a pit about 6ft (1.9m) deep, 10ft (3m) long and 4ft (1.2m) wide. A log was laid lengthwise over it and two men with a long saw cut it into planks and beams, one standing on top of the log and the other in the pit.

Trees were sawn up in the woods to reduce weight. Itinerant sawyers would spend the winter producing planks etc using the brick lined and covered pits in wheelwright and builders' yards. In the summer they would move around the wooded estates cutting fence posts, beams etc in temporary pits in the woods. Sometimes a particularly large tree would have a pit dug underneath it where it lay after felling.

8. Down Wood. *Down* in this case means *hill*. This is a hazel coppice with oak standards. The girth of the oak trees indicates at least two periods of planting, the oldest are about 8'8" (2.7m) in girth giving an age of about 150 years. The bluebells and other plants also show that this is an ancient wood.

9. Potash Pit. These shallow pits are likely to have been used to burn the waste twigs etc resulting from coppicing and forestry to make potash. The papery ash was soaked in water and the water was then drawn off as *lye* for use as a washing liquid and to make soap. The residue was added to sand as a flux to reduce the temperature at which the sand melted when making glass. Different trees produced different colours, beech gave pink, elm – blue etc.

10. Potash kiln. As well as being used for washing and glass making, potash was also made in larger quantities for use as agricultural fertiliser, particularly as a top-dressing for grassland. In the Kennet Valley peat was burned to make potash, but away from the valley wood and bracken were used.

Guidance. This pit is about 200 yards to the right along the wide track. It lies just beyond the bank and is marked by a large holly tree.

11. Permitted Paths. The Gerald Palmer Trust has a very generous policy of allowing public access to many of its wood and farm tracks. Look for the green map boards and waymarks. The bridleway crossing here was created as part of Eling Farm's Higher Level Stewardship Plan and is open to walkers as well as riders.

12. Pheasant Release Pens These pens are used to accustom young pheasants to life in the wild before they are released in the late summer. Pheasant shooting is the reason for the survival of so many small areas of woodland and coppice. Without a function as pheasant cover the woods would have been cleared and converted to agriculture long ago

Roman settlement. A Roman farm existed in the fields to the east of this path. It was the ancestor of the Saxon farm and demonstrates the long term continuity of farming in the Pang Valley. It was fully excavated in the 19th century and the finds dispersed and lost. **The site is a Scheduled Ancient**

Monument which it is an offence to damage or disturb in any way.
13. Eling Farm. This is an ancient site. The name is in an early form of Anglo Saxon meaning the *place of Eli's people*. The estate belonged to the Saxon royal family and was probably a sub-unit of a larger estate based on Hampstead Norreys. In

Eling Farm barns.

Domesday Book it was held by Roger de Ivry and it only had four ploughs indicating about 120 acres of arable. It had wood for 30 pigs which is quite a lot of woodland. In 1761 it was in Eeling Green on the edge of Ealing (Hampstead Norreys) Common. The Common was enclosed in 1778. The farm buildings were built in the mid 19th century. Today it is the centre of an organic farm rented from the Eling Estate by the Goodenough family who have been farming here since the 1920's. More details are given above.

14. Chalk pit. The soils overlying the chalk bedrock are often too acid to grow cereals. The early farmer's remedy was to dig through to the chalk and then to spread large quantities of it on the fields where it was allow it to weather before being ploughed in. This had to be repeated at regular intervals and there are many chalk pits in fields and woods. The modern farmer uses lime, which is half the weight of chalk, made by burning limestone.

15. Everington Barn. Although this is without doubt an 18th century wheat barn it is not shown on the maps of 1773 and 1845. Barns of this type were constructed of pre-fabricated timber frames and could be dismantled and rebuilt fairly easily. This barn must have been moved from somewhere else, probably Everington.

16. Hedge Line. This hedge is shown in 1773 and is probably many hundred of years old. Note the large lynchet which has been created by plough loosened soil building against the up-hill side and by soil moving away from the downhill side.

17. The River Pang. This is a chalk *bourne* meaning that it often dries up for part of the year. After a wet winter the head of the West Pang is East Ilsley pond and the North Pang rises on Churn Plain. They join at Compton. The

St Abbs bathing place   With acknowledgements to Mrs Smart

perennial head is at the Blue Pools between Stanford Dingley and Bradfield. The whole of Chapter Eight is dedicated to describing the wildlife of this interesting river.

18. The Swimming Pool. In the early 1930's the then Prince of Wales, who became Edward VIII but who abdicated before his coronation, appealed for landowners to provide more sporting and leisure facilities for the population. Mr TC Dewe of Everington Farm responded by building the pool and by providing a camping site and three tennis courts. Using the pool cost 6d (2.5p) for a private changing cubicle and 3d if the communal changing room was used. The pool was 6 feet (1.8m) deep at one end and 3 feet (0.9m) deep at the other. As a reward for his public spirited action the local authority increased his rates and so he closed the site in 1938. It continued to be used unofficially for many years.

19. St Abb's Orchard. An orchard is shown on this site in 1773. The trees have been identified as *Pott's Seedling, Blenheim Orange, Bramley's Seedling* and *Lord Derby*. These were all developed in the mid 19th century

20. St Abbs. St Abb was the 7th century Saxon Abbess of a nunnery in Kent. She also gave her name to the area called St Ebb's in Oxford. Frilsham church is dedicated to St Frideswide, another Saxon female saint associated with Oxford. Oxford was first fortified by King Alfred the Great who owned the Pang Valley and there is clearly a link between the Pang Valley and Oxford.

21. Parish Boundary. Parish boundaries are often the boundaries of early Saxon estates and were usually fixed by the 9th century AD. This lane has been here for at least 1000 years and probably much longer.

Sources and further reading

Victoria County History – Berkshire

Morris J (Ed)	*Domesday Book – Berkshire* Phillimore 1979	
Wood M	*Domesday – a search for the roots of England* BBC 1986	
Ekwall E (ed)	*The Concise Dictionary of English Place-names* OUP 1974	
Mabey R	*Flora Britannica* Chatto & Windus 1997	
Greenaway D & Ward D (Eds)	*In the Valley of the Pang* 2002	
Williamson T	*Shaping Medieval Landscapes* Windgather Press 2003	
Chapman R	*A Record of the History & Inhabitants of Hampstead Norreys Parish* 1990	
Winchester A	*Discovering Parish Boundaries* Shire Publications 2000	

CHAPTER SIX

New paths and old boundaries
Ashampstead Common and Upper Basildon

Veteran Ash

Commons. There can be few words in the English language as widely misunderstood as the word *Commons*. Most people would understand the word to mean 'land owned by the community to which everyone has a right of access', and they would be quite wrong! Commons are land owned by one person over which other specified people (commoners) have defined rights. Many commons were wood pastures where only those people who had Right of Common could graze their animals, gather firewood, cut bracken for animal bedding and exercise other similar rights. There were several other types of common including water areas and moorland grazing.

Commons were not just waste ground. They were an important resource and essential to the farming system. They allowed animals to be grazed during the summer so that the meadows could be used to grow hay to feed the animals in winter. It was particularly important to keep the plough oxen well fed so that the spring ploughing went well. The lack of ploughing and the grazing produced a special and valuable flora on the commons and preserved many archaeological features.

Deer Parks were both practical deer farms to supply fresh meat and the ultimate status symbol for the medieval land owner. They were very expensive to create and maintain and usually a Grant of Free Warren had to be obtained before they could be built. The park pale at Ashampstead Common is more than 3½ miles long and consists of a large bank with a deep ditch on the inside. Originally it would have had an oak paling fence or a hedge along the top.

To manage the park and to combat poachers, two parkers were employed and provided with houses from which they could watch the deer and the roads into the park. A pond was dug to water the deer and a park lane created around the perimeter to allow maintenance of the fence. The deer were usually fallow deer, introduced by the Normans from Sicily and less prone to escaping than our native deer.

Pillow Mounds. Rabbits were another introduced animal kept in parks. Pillow mounds are artificial warrens. Rabbits were present in Britain before the last Ice Age but did not return with the other mammals when the ice retreated. They are first recorded as being kept in the Scilly Isles in the 12th century and in 1135 Drake's Island in Plymouth Sound was granted to Plympton Priory 'with the rabbits'.

Rabbits were delicate and expensive creatures, valued both for their flesh and for their fur which was used to trim and line winter clothing. In the 13th century a single rabbit would have cost a workman more than a day's pay. Because of their high value rabbit warrens were the target of organised crime and there are records of attacks on warreners' houses by armed gangs. The houses were strongly built to resist such attacks and some of them look like small forts.

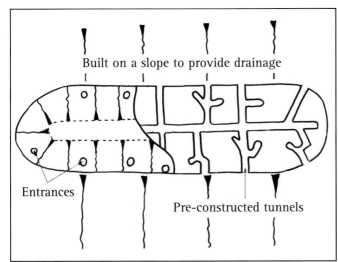

Built on a slope to provide drainage

Entrances

Pre-constructed tunnels

Diagram of a Pillow Mound

Saxon Charters and Boundaries. From about the 7th century AD until the Norman Conquest in 1066 the Saxon inhabitants of Southern Britain developed a very efficient civil and legal system. All major land transfers were documented with charters setting out the boundaries of the land being transferred and any duties, rights and privileges attached to it. These boundaries can sometimes be identified and part of this walk runs along a boundary detailed in about 880AD when King Alfred exchanged land with the Bishop of Winchester.

Veteran Trees for the Future. Britain has by far the largest collection of ancient trees of any European country except Greece. We have oak pollards which have been alive since the Norman Conquest and yew trees that were already ancient when the Romans invaded. However, they will not last for ever and it is important that the next generation of ancients is identified for our descendants to appreciate and wonder at.

Ancient and veteran trees are trees with a story to tell and experience to share. They tell stories of their lives, of the countryside in which they were planted. They tell how they supplied the surrounding communities with some of the essentials of life such as fuel, timber to build homes and wood for tools. In addition to this their scars and rugged bark provide homes and sustenance for myriads of creatures from tiny invertebrates to birds and mammals.

Veteran Trees for the Future, ancient sweet chestnut pollards

To provide the next generation, Yattendon Estates has set aside 22 trees scattered over Ashampstead and Burnt Hill Commons and these will be managed to preserve them for the future. They have all been marked and recorded, and a management plan has been established for each one. A leaflet has been published to introduce the trees to walkers and it has been heartening to see family groups out 'hunting for the trees', leaflet in hand.

This walk includes Ashampstead Common and Buckhold
It starts and finishes at Childs Court Farm

- It is about 3½ miles or 5.6 km long. The route is along wide, clear and well marked tracks.
- There are three hills and surfaces can be uneven and muddy.
- There are two short lengths of road walking and four road crossings.
- Horses and riders may be encountered.

Ordnance Survey map Explorer 158 'Newbury and Hungerford' will be useful.

1. Childs Court Farm. This is a carefully designed farm complex built to serve the surrounding fields when they were enclosed in about 1680. Before that they were Open Fields farmed in strips.

The large barn was for wheat; bread was the population's staple food. In the 1920's it became a milking parlour. The farm supplied TB tested milk to London hospitals. The smaller barn was for barley which was used to make malt. Beer was the usual drink before the introduction of tea, even for children. This barn has now been converted for use as an office.

Child's Court Farm about 1930

A 14th century open hall house

2. 14th century house. This house is built on four arches made of curved oak trees. When new it was open to the roof and had no chimney. The fire was on the floor and the smoke found its own way out!

3. A devious road. The local Methodists requested a wide road to allow them to get to the chapel at Quicks Green with clean shoes. However, the Lord of the Manor (an Anglican) was only prepared to grant a narrow footpath. So the farmer at Childs Court (a Methodist) piled the gravel 2 yards wide and 3 feet

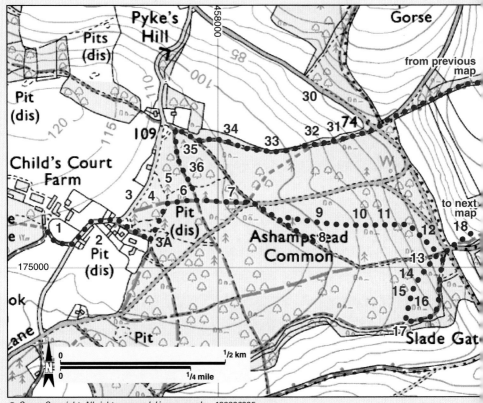

high. Nature took a hand and the pile slipped sideways and provided the wide path originally requested. The Lord of the Manor's comments are not recorded!

Guidance note: Walk down the gravelled Restricted Byway and into the wood opposite 'The Forge'. Note the veteran sweet chestnut on your left. Sixty metres from the entrance fork left along The Kids' Path which curves left past another veteran sweet chestnut and joins a major ride at Point 4 after a few metres. Turn right along this ride.

3A. Veteran Trees for the Future. A special leaflet has been produced describing these trees and other magnificent trees on the Commons. The scheme is described in the first part of this chapter.

4. Old road. This was the original road to the farm; Yattendon Lane was actually a turning off this road. Old maps show this track as a conifer lined avenue.

5. Exotic trees. The owner in the late 19th century planted exotic trees in many parts of the Common. His forester had to plant by stealth because the

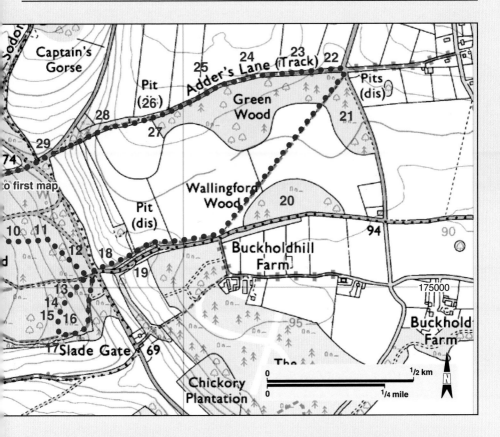

commoners objected to the new trees and set boys to trail him and to pull up the saplings! Look for wellingtonias, a monkey puzzle tree, cedars of Lebanon and many others.

6. Standing deadwood. The plan for managing these woods recognises the value to wildlife of deadwood. It provides homes for many fungi, insects and invertebrates. These are the bottom of the food chain and provide food for many other creatures. **Without dead wood a wood is dead!**

7. World War 2. During the war the army used the woods to hide soldiers during the build up to D Day in 1944. The troops lived under canvas but cook houses and latrines were built. They were later knocked down and their bases are slowly disappearing as soil builds over them, just as it covered Roman buildings 2000 years ago.

8. Holly. Holly leaves have the highest nutritional value of any tree leaf and holly was grown as fodder for deer, sheep and cattle. The branches were cut in early summer and stored in ricks. They were fed to the animals in winter.

Medieval ladies ferreting rabbits from a pillow mound   with acknowledgements to the British Library

The animals stripped the leaves and the bark and the denuded twigs were then used as firewood. Nothing was wasted! Repeated cutting produces these holly rings which are actually one tree and hundreds of years old.

9. Yews. The Commons have many different soils. This area is a chalky Icknield soil which yews like. The larger ones are probably 500 years old. They were not used for bows; the best yew for bows came from the mountains in north Spain.

10. Coppiced beech. This ancient tree is notable because beech does not coppice easily.

11. Pillow Mound. This is an artificial rabbit warren. They are often found in deer parks. Rabbits were imported from southern Europe in the 12th century. They did not naturally burrow and found our climate harsh so warrens were built for them. Their flesh and fur were very valuable; the fur was used to line winter clothing and in the 19th century was mixed with glue to make top hats.

12. Sweet chestnut. These are true natives, the horse chestnut is not. It is possible that the Romans imported sweet chestnut, but its charcoal has been

Pang Valley Conservation Volunteers working on Buckhold Meadow.

found on many early sites. The trees at this site started to grow about 1850 when grazing of the commons declined and allowed saplings to get established.

13. Buckhold Glade. This is on chalky Icknield soil. Look for wild strawberries, marjoram, great mullein, St John's wort. This is one of three glades cut and cleared every year by The Pang Valley Conservation Volunteers.

14. Ian's Path. This is a new path named for Ian Stephan, the consultant responsible for Yattendon Estate's Woodland Plan whose suggestion it was.

15. Chalk Pit. This is a small example. There are many very large pits in other parts of the commons and in other woods and fields. The chalk was spread on the acid soils in fields to raise their pH. so that cereals could be grown. Although they overlie chalk many soils around the area are very acid – particularly just after they have been cleared from woodland.

16. Windblow. This area was devastated by the hurricanes of 1990. Replanting brought large amounts of chalk to the surface which has encouraged a rich chalk land flora.

17. Deer Park pale. This was built just before 1240 by John of Bagpuize, Lord of the Manor of Bradfield. It had a fence or a hedge on the top. In 1236 the Statute of Merton recognised that the woodland resource was being dangerously over exploited and allowed Lords of Manors to enclose manorial waste being used as pasture provided they left 'sufficient' for their tenants. This resulted in many pasture woods being enclosed with banks and ditches and used as deer parks or as intensively managed coppices.

Deer park pale built about 1240.

18. New Permitted Bridleway. This was created in 2004. Yattendon Estates leased the land for 10 years, West Berkshire Council and the Ramblers Association provided

A park pale fence of the medieval pattern

the materials, and Rob Ward, who farms Buckhold Hill Farm, erected the fences. The PVCV facilitated the project.

19. Buckhold Hill. Early English had many names for 'valley' and used them to describe the type of valley accurately. *Hold* meant a steep sided valley. The only native buck is the roebuck, so the name means 'the steep sided valley of the roebuck'. This matches one of the landmarks on the 880AD charter of King Alfred transferring land in Basildon to the Bishop of Winchester.

20. Wallingford Wood. This is only about 100 years old. The old maple stool is probably a survivor of an earlier hedge.

21. Green Wood. This also is a recent plantation and is not shown on the Ordnance Survey map of 1877.

22. Adder Lane. In 1877 this was called 'Odours Lane'. Early OS surveyors were instructed to take great care in recording names. However, they usually questioned the educated who may have gentrified the names! The lane is the boundary between Basildon and Bradfield parishes and this means it is likely to have existed in the 9th century AD. This and other clues make it probably another part of the boundary in Alfred's charter. In other parts of the country similar boundaries have been shown to be much older and to have used Roman and even Iron Age boundary features.

23. Ancient ash stool. A girth of 5.26m indicates an age of at least 300 years. It was last cut about 1950.

24. True crab apple tree. Many wild apple trees are the result of discarded apple cores. True crab trees are not common. This is also evidently an ancient tree.

25. Old field maple stool. This is 5.87m in girth indicating an age of over 300 years.

26. Chalk pit. As at No.15, chalk from this pit was used to sweeten the acid clays of surrounding fields.

27. Standing deadwood. Note the bracket fungi and numerous holes in this large beech stump. It is providing food and shelter for millions – probably billions – of organisms.

28. Yews. Once again yews become the dominant tree as the chalk comes

300 year old field maple stool.

close to the surface. Although interesting as our longest lived tree, their dense shade does not permit anything to live beneath them. Shakespeare considered it a 'poisonous shade'.

29. Wych Elm Bottom. An ancient wych elm grew here. Legend has it that a meeting of Ashampstead witches and Basildon witches on Basildon Heath broke up in violence and the Ashampstead party were chased down Adder Lane by the Basildon coven. On reaching the boundary, and being fortified by his own land, the chief Ashampstead witch stuck his staff in the ground and hurled a spell at his pursuers which sent them back in disarray. His staff took root and became the 'witch elm'. When it collapsed in the late 19th century it was full of wild bees' nests and people came with buckets from miles around to collect the honey.

30. The Saxon Boundary. This probably continued along the bottom of the valley to the next landmark which was a farm. This may have been on the site of Pyt House which is itself an ancient building.

31. WW2 and park pale. This is the base of a cook house. The bank and ditch are one of the better preserved parts of the 13th century deer park boundary.

32. Chalk pit and scour lines. Another example of a chalk quarry. The deeply cut paths are due to feet, hooves and wheels eroding the soil over centuries of use.

33. Possibly another pillow mound.

Rich ground flora produced by centuries of lack of ground disturbance

34. Ancient Yew. At 5.41m girth this yew is at least 600 years old. It is growing on the park pale which must therefore have gone out of use by the 15th century – possibly as a result of the Black Death in 1348/9. Basildon manor records say that no rents were collected at this time because all the tenants were dead.

35. Lime stool. This great tree fell in the 1990 gales. The re-growth is a good example of coppicing. It will eventually form a ring of stems.

36. Birch Glade. This open area was one of several new glades created by Yattendon Estates as part of a twenty year woodland management agreement.

Ancient yew on the park pale bank

Sources and further reading

Victoria County History – Berkshire

Morris J (Ed)	*Domesday Book – Berkshire* Phillimore 1979
Wood M	*Domesday – a search for the roots of England* BBC 1986
Ekwall E (ed)	*The Concise Dictionary of English Place-names* OUP 1974
Mabey R	*Flora Britannica* Chatto & Windus 1997
Williamson T	*Shaping Medieval Landscapes* Windgather Press 2003
Williamson T	*The Archaeology of Rabbit Warrens* Shire Publications 2006
Greenaway D & Ward D (Eds)	*In the Valley of the Pang* Priately Published 2002
Greenaway, D	*The Commons of Ashampstead Parish* Ashampstead Parish Council 1998
Rackham O.	*The History of the Countryside* Dent 1986
	Veteran Trees for the Future Friends of the Pang, Kennet & Lambourn Valleys 2005

CHAPTER SEVEN

Ancient and Modern
Yattendon and Burnt Hill

Burnt Hill Reservoir
DW. 2.5.07

The Development of the Village People have lived in and around Yattendon for thousands of years. A Mesolithic stone tool known as a Thames Pick dating from between 10,000 and 4,500BC, was found at Coombe House on the edge of the village. A Bronze Age burial mound exists in the corner of the parish at Everington. A Roman farmhouse was excavated on Eling Farm in the 19th century and the Manor of Yattendon was recorded in Domesday Book in 1086. The Domesday record says that the land had been owned by the Saxon royal family.

It is probable that Yattendon and Frilsham were once a single Saxon estate. The original boundary between them looks very contrived whereas the outer boundary is purposeful and forms an almost complete circle. The dividing line steps around medieval strips and Yattendon Great Field is actually in Frilsham!

Yattendon means *The Hollow of the People of Geat* and this hollow, and the original settlement, was probably around the modern school. The oldest pottery has been found in this area. When the Manor and the Square were built in the 15th century the focus of the village moved up to the Square. In the 17th century we have records of a Yattendon grocer striking his own tokens.

The first Yattendon Court 1879.

The Norreys Family. The Norys family of Bray acquired the manor of Yattendon by marriage in the early 15th century. In 1448 John Norris obtained a licence to build and fortify the manor house. He built it astride the road to Hampstead Norreys and diverted the road through a new market place in the Square. He also built the present church, although there was almost certainly an earlier church in the village and it was probably on the same site.

The Norreys were an important and aggressive political family and their exploits read like the more lurid kind of historical fiction. Sir William Norreis was knighted on the battlefield of Northampton (19 July 1458) and Sir Henry Norris was executed for an alleged, but unlikely, *affaire* with Queen Anne Boleyn. His son, Sir John Norreys, was a mercenary soldier and in 1573 he joined the Earl of Essex in an attempt to colonise Ulster. He was known as 'Black Jack' Norreys and In 1577 he sailed with Sir Francis Drake to attack the Macdonnell stronghold on Rathlin Island. After a two day siege the defenders were overwhelmed and every man, woman and child on the island was massacred. After three months the island was abandoned.

The Waterhouse Era. Alfred Waterhouse and his wife Elizabeth bought the manor in 1877. Alfred Waterhouse was a famous Victorian architect. Amongst other buildings, he designed the Natural History Museum in London and Reading Town Hall. The Waterhouses made many changes to the village; some of these are noted in the walk paragraphs. Elizabeth Waterhouse taught young village people to make brass and copper items to her designs. These were then sold in a village shop and at Liberty's in London. They won many prizes for their work.

The Modern Estate. The Waterhouse family sold the estate to Sir Edward Iliffe in 1925 and the Iliffe family have continued the process of maintaining and improving the village. Again, a number of their changes are noted in the walk paragraphs. They increased the size of the estate to 8923 acres of which 2181 acres are woodland. There is a very modern dairy unit which manages 550 cows and 220 young animals. A variety of arable crops are grown ranging from wheat and barley, through beans and oil seed rape to opium poppies for the pharmaceutical industry. Redundant farm buildings have been converted into workshops and offices which provide local employment.

The Withys. Yattendon Estate provided the land for these twelve houses in 1990 and they were built by the English Villages Housing Association (EVHA), which aims to keep young people in the countryside by providing affordable housing in areas which would otherwise be beyond the pockets of most young couples. Four houses are rented and managed by the Sovereign Housing Association. The other eight are sold with EVHA retaining 40% of the equity. The owners buy the remaining 60% using a normal mortgage. They are thus able to build up their investment and move on to better things, selling the house back to EVHA for another young local couple to buy. That is the theory! But in practice this is such a good place to live that people rarely move on!

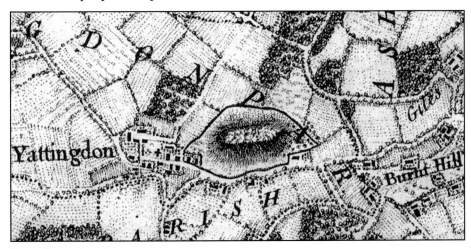

The walk area in 1761

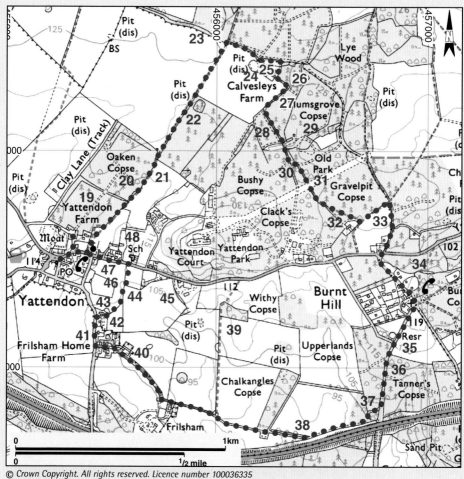

**This walk includes Yattendon Village and Burnt Hill.
It starts and finishes in Yattendon Square.**

- It is about 4 miles or 6 km long. The route is along wide, clear and well marked tracks.
- Surfaces can be uneven and muddy.
- There are three road crossings and two lengths of roads to walk along where there are no pavements .
- Farm vehicles and equipment share some of the paths.
- Horses and riders may be encountered.

Ordnance Survey map Explorer 158 'Newbury and Hungerford' will be useful.

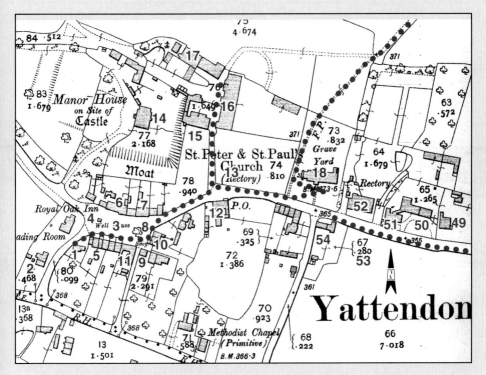

1. The Carriers. This car park was the carriers' yard. Carriers were the ancestors of our rural bus services. They travelled fixed routes to a published timetable using a wagon and horses and carried both goods and people. They also undertook shopping commissions for people and would shop for the most trivial items such as buttons and pots and pans.

2. The Reading Room. (Now a private house called The Close). The Waterhouse family were originally Quakers and disapproved of alcohol. They built and staffed a Reading Room which provided books and the latest newspapers and served the best coffee and cakes for miles around.

The carrier and his equipment on the site of the car park 1898

3. The Square. This appears to have been deliberately built as a market place in the 15th century although there had been markets in the village from the 13th century. Saddlers Cottage dates from at least the 15th century and may be older.

Yattendon Square and Fete in 1907

4. The well. Waterborne diseases were common in the days before piped water. The Waterhouses had the well dug in 1878 to supply safe drinking water. It is 131' (39.9m) deep and cost £29.65.

5. The Barracks. Parliamentarian troops are reputed to have been billeted in these houses during the Civil War (1642–46), hence the name. Note the chimneys. These and the steepness of the roofs show that the houses were originally thatched.

6. The Royal Oak. An 18th century false front makes this building look more modern than The Barracks, but they are actually of the same date. Again, note the chimneys. In 1785, Robert States, the landlord of the Royal Oak, took over the Yattendon Kiln and advertised its products in the *Reading Mercury.* The left hand end of the range was once the village abbatoir.

7. The hairdresser's salon. This was used by The Home Arts & Industries organisation to sell the Yattendon Copper and Brass made by Elizabeth Waterhouse's pupils.

8. The tree. A tree is shown here on the earliest map (1773). A very ancient elm died here during the Dutch Elm epidemic of the early 1970s and was replaced with an oak by Lord Iliffe in 1977.

9. The forge. *Eustache the smith* is recorded in 1315 and a forge would have been an essential part of the village until recent times. Forge Cottage has an inscribed date of 1675 but the forge is 19th century. The Briant family were the smiths in the 18th & 19th century and gave their name to the lane. Two female members are recorded as smiths. They were succeeded by the Prints at the end of the 19th century.

10. The fire engine. In the early 1900's this shed held the manual fire engine.

11. The Stores. Maps of 1773 and 1845 show this as an open site, but a shop had been built by 1877 when it was destroyed in a fire. Alfred Waterhouse

The fire engine and its crew about 1910.

bought the ruins, re-built the shop and leased it back to the former owner.

12. Bakery, brewery and green phone box. This was the village bakery and is now the headquarters of the world famous West Berkshire Brewery. The identity of the painters who painted the phone box green is a closely guarded local secret!

13. The Village Hall. It was built by the first Lord Iliffe in 1931 at a cost of £1250 and has been central to village life ever since.

14. The Manor House. A fortified manor house surrounded by a moat was built here in 1448. It sat astride the original road to Hampstead Norris and the slight holloways marking the old road and the extension of Clay Lane could still be seen in the grounds until recently. The first phase of the present house was built about 1680 but it has been extended, refaced and remodelled several times since then.

15. The Grange. A date on the chimney indicates that this was built in 1702 by Sir Edward Norreys, probably for his estate manager since it backs onto the farmyard and the manor barns.

16. The Manor Wheat Barn. This is an magnificent eleven bay timber framed barn and was probably built at the same time as the fortified manor house in 1448. It was originally thatched and without side aisles. Slots for wattle panels can be seen in the main posts. Graffiti on the end wall may indicate that it was extended and tiled before 1743. The barn is often wrongly called a *Tithe Barn.* Tithe Barns were used by the Church to house the Tithe. This was a tax of one tenth levied in kind on the increase of the land. It was intended to support the Church, but it was often abused and in the mid 19th century it was commuted for a cash payment.

17. The Manor Barley Barn. This is smaller than the wheat barn reflecting the relative importance of the crops. Wheat made bread, 'the staff of life' before the introduction of the potato. Barley made malt for beer. Important but not vital!

Guidance: Now retrace your steps to the main road and turn left.

Yattendon church before the Waterhouse restoration.

A scratch dial for timing services.

18. The church. John Norreys claimed to have built the church *de novo* (from new) in about 1450 but the list of rectors goes back to 1297 so there was certainly an earlier church in the village. It was probably on the same site. There is a remarkable monument to Sir John Norreys in the church which included his helmet until it was stolen.

Look for the scratch dial on the buttress close to the west of the small priest's door. This sundial allowed the acolyte to time the sermons!

The church has been remodelled several times, most recently by the Waterhouse family in the late 19th century. The red sandstone cross in the front church yard is a memorial to the mother of Robert Bridges, who lived in Yattendon Manor and married a daughter of Alfred Waterhouse. He was appointed Poet Laureate in 1913.

Guidance: Walk around the west side of the church and through the rear churchyard to a gate in the north boundary. Turn right and follow the path.

19. Brick Close. This is shown as open land in 1773 and 1877. It seems to have been the kiln site for clay dug from a quarry in Yattendon Park. In spring the lack of bluebells and the generally impoverished flora is noticeable.

20. Oaken Copse. This copse demonstrates the concept of Ancient Woodland Indicators (Chapter 4). In Spring it is thick with bluebells and it also contains many other less dramatic indicators.

21. Yattendon Park. John Norreys was granted the right to make a deer park here in the 15th century. The modern park covers some of his park and contains many ancient trees. The park pale runs NE along the hedge from near the school. The white cattle are British Whites, a Rare Breed.

One of the few surviving Methodist chapels   *Dr Watneys' reservoir*

22. Chalk Quarry. Chalk from this large pit was used to sweeten the acid soils in the surrounding fields.

23. Ambrose Row. This line of trees hides an ancient road.

24. Chalk pits. Note the partly filled pits either side of the track.

25. Calvesleys. The name means *grazing land for calves.* The 1773 map shows a small field with narrow shelter belts of trees on three sides. The barns and houses are 19th century and were called Nersham's Homestead.

26. Pig Unit. This is one of three originally built by Yattendon Estate. They were leased to specialist pig farmers in the late 1990's when the devastating fall in pork prices made them uneconomic as part of a mixed farm.

27. Christmas Trees. Yattendon Estate is one of the largest private producers of Christmas trees in Britain. The species grown are Norway spruce and *abies normanianna.* There are several hundred acres of plantations and about 70-80,000 trees are sold every year.

28. Pond. This is shown on a map of 1773 and has recently been extended. It drains into a swallow hole to the east of the path.

29. Sawmill. The bricks for the first Yattendon Court were made here.

30. Exotic pests. The bamboo and *rhododendron ponticum* planted in the Court gardens are now a major pest.

31. The Avenue. Legend has it that this was planned as an escape runway for the first Lord Iliffe should the Nazis have invaded Britain! It is actually a 'vista' . The then Lord Iliffe made a virtue out of a necessity when he had to cut a large number of trees to fulfil a wartime demand for timber. The horse chestnuts were planted by the girls of a school evacuated here during World War 2 and they were originally marked with the girls' names.

32. Old Park. These houses were built in the 1930's and were originally thatched. They were on the site of an Isolation Hospital built by Elizabeth Waterhouse during a scarlet fever epidemic in the village. It was later used as a convalescent hospital for invalid members of staff by the Huntley & Palmer biscuit company of Reading.

33. Ancient road. This is also the parish boundary and was probably in existence in the 9th century. The area's name *Challengehook* means *disputed bend.*

The chalk mines with acknowledgements to Ross Stewart

34. Burnt Hill. This was a brick making settlement in the 18th & 19th centuries and it may have got its name from the glow in the night sky caused by the kilns. The chapel was built in 1864 and is still in use. There was a convoy camp here during World War 2.

35. Reservoir. This was part of the water supply scheme built by Dr Watney of Buckhold in 1906/07.

19th century graffitti.
with acknowledgements to Ross Stewart

There were other reservoirs in Greathouse Wood and at Tutt's Clump. When full, this one holds 500,000 gallons (c.2.5million litres)and the water is 11feet (3.3m) deep. The concrete base was built by 43 men in five days using ballast and sand dug on the Estate. The reservoir cost £3,509.

36. Roadside Nature Reserve. Established for common spotted orchids.

37. Original road. This track is part of the original road to Stanford Dingley and it was cut off when the M4 was built.

38. Permitted bridleway. Granted by Yattendon Estate to link to the Right of Way to Home Farm.

39. The chalk pit and mines. As with the other pits on this walk, the chalk was used to sweeten the soil. The mines provided chalk to add to the clays and sands used to make bricks. Graffiti in the mines are reported to go back to 1720. The tunnels were large enough to take a pony and cart. The

The modern dairy unit commissioned in 2002

Frilsham Home Farm. A 19th century planned farmstead

entrances were closed in about 1930. One tunnel was provided with a steel door and kept as a cool food store for Yattendon Court. It is now a bat roost.

40. The dairy unit. Commissioned on 2 September 2002, it is designed to handle 550 milking cows and 220 young stock. It uses the most up to date computer controls and sensors. It is supported by 735 acres of land growing 60% maize and 40% grass. It produces 4.7 million litres of milk a year, enough to supply a daily pint to everyone in a town of 22,500 people.

41. Frilsham Home Farm. The redundant buildings of this late 19th century model farm have been converted into business units.

42. The Withys. The name is taken from a wood, Withys Copse, near the field in which the houses were built; it means willow coppice. Willow was used for making baskets and for holding thatch on to roofs and ricks long before it was used for cricket bats.

43. Quarry pit. This is another pit which supplied chalk to sweeten the surrounding soils.

44. Old road. Look at the old map dated 1761 included in this chapter. It shows a lane running along this hedge to the old village site near the modern school. The bank and its species-richness indicate that it is an ancient hedge.

45. Brick making. The land to the east is noticeably lower and the Estate Office is standing on a distinct promontory. The lowering was caused by digging clay, sand and chalk to make bricks. The kiln was on the Estate

Office site and was already in existence in 1785 when Robert States, the landlord of the Royal Oak, took it over.

46. Ancient ash tree. This splendid veteran tree is 5.15m in girth and is probably at least 300 years old. Pollards were cut off about 3m above the ground and allowed to re-shoot out of reach of browsing animals. They were cut at

Yattendon School as newly built in 1886

regular intervals to provide timber and firewood and this lopping has caused the scarring.

47. Pond. This is fed by a spring emerging from under the hill. It was part of the water supply for the old village. Another spring just beyond the Estate Office was known as the Miraculous Well because it never failed.

48. The school. The Howard family were lords of the manor in the 19th century and they provided a school near the rectory. The present school and the adjoining teacher's house were built in 1886 by the Waterhouse family at their own expense. It was designed to hold 110 pupils but usually had about 80. The noise must have been deafening!

49. Nurse's House. St Martin's was built in 1909 to house the village nurse and as a memorial to Alfred Waterhouse.

50. Malt Barn Cottages. These were built using the bricks and timbers from demolished Lower Farm farm buildings.

51. Malthouse. This was originally Lower Farm, (the upper farm being the manor farm). It farmed the land to the east of the village.

52. Old Rectory. A document of 1608 shows that an earlier medieval rectory existed on this site before the first phase of the present house was built in 1747. This house was extended by building another house against it. This was discovered during the refurbishment work in 2004.

53. The Tithe Barn. The 1608 document makes it clear that this was in the field opposite the rectory where buildings are shown on a map of 1773. The Tithe Barn held the rector's tithe. This was a tax in kind of a tenth of the increase of the land intended to support the church. It was commuted for a cash payment in the 19th century. The barn was burned down in the late

19th century and only the uneven surface marks the spot.
54. Isaac's. This is a 15/16th century jettied house. Note the small medieval windows close under the eaves. These *wind holes* were originally unglazed and covered with wooden shutters. The steepness of the roof shows that it was originally thatched. It was probably tiled in the 18th or 19th century.

Sources and further reading

Victoria County History – Berkshire

Morris J (Ed)	*Domesday Book – Berkshire* Phillimore 1979
Wood M	*Domesday – a search for the roots of England* BBC 1986
Ekwall E (ed)	*The Concise Dictionary of English Place-names* OUP 1974
Mabey R	*Flora Britannica* Chatto & Windus 1997
Williamson T	*Shaping Medieval Landscapes* Windgather Press 2003
Greenaway D & Ward D (Eds)	*In the Valley of the Pang* The Friends of Pang & Kennet Valleys 2002
Greenaway D	*Yattendon for Visitors* Privately published 2004
Rackham O	*The History of the Countryside* Dent 1986
Natural England	*Ancient Woodland Vascular Plants.*

CHAPTER EIGHT

The River

The River Pang, its geology and wildlife

Ben McFarland

Old Boys' Bathing Place
BW. 11-7-07

The geology. The River Pang is an excellent example of a chalk stream. Through a combination of the special geology, climate and indeed human activity, chalk streams have developed features that are unique.

Chalk is a soft, porous rock that only occurs in Northern Europe, North America and New Zealand. Rainfall percolates into the chalk and is slowly discharged into the river, stabilising temperature and filtering the water. The downland catchments sustain moderately fast flowing streams enabling the water to remain well oxygenated. Oxygen rich water, together with the stable flows, temperature and mineral rich waters, result in an excellent diversity of plants and animals.

The history of the river. Many of the features we see today associated with a chalk stream such as the Pang, are actually a result of man's activities.

Thousands of years ago the Pang would have drained a heavily shaded catchment, dominated by trees such as oak and beech on the slopes with willow and alder woods along the damp valley bottoms. It is possible that the Pang flowed along several channels, at least for part of its length, and most of these would have been heavily shaded by trees. Consequently there would have been less weed growth within the channel, especially in the narrower upper reaches, and most of the plant material in the river would have been derived from leaf fall.

By the Roman Period, most of the trees had been felled, opening up the river to sunlight. Consequently many of the animals thriving in the rich growth of aquatic plants that now exist along the length of the Pang, may have been scarce. One example is the Grannon *(Brachycentrus subnubilis)*, a caddisfly which attaches its case to the flowing fronds of water-crowfoot.

In more recent times flows on many chalk streams have been modified by water mills. These have significantly altered the habitat, creating areas of artificially slow 'ponded' water and fast gravel glides.

River Pang at Frilsham 1995

The former forested valley floor was drained and turned into water meadows through complex systems of channels and sluices which enabled controlled flooding to increase grass growth for sheep. Most of these water meadows have now been lost due to agricultural intensification.

As with nearly every river in lowland Britain, the Pang has lost a lot of connectivity with the floodplain through channel engineering as man has tried to control flooding and increase agricultural productivity. This has reduced the diversity of floodplain habitats. Fortunately the Pang has retained many natural features within the channel itself.

The same channel in 1992

Kingfisher   *Heron*
The photographs above are with acknowledgements to the Environment Agency

The numbers of different animals and plants within the channel and banks are greatly enhanced by the diversity of physical features. Examples of these include eroding cliffs, fallen trees, marginal shelves, gravel riffles, deeper pools and in-stream islands. Each feature provides habitat for a different set of species. Eroding earth cliffs, for example, which are often found on the outside of bends (meanders) in the river, can provide the ideal conditions for a kingfisher nest site. In-stream islands provide security from predators and are often very rich in wildlife. They can range from temporary features that will wash away during the next flood, to permanent islands with mature trees.

The plant community. Like many chalk streams, the Pang has a reasonably diverse plant community. Along the margins of the river and in wetter parts of the valley, sedges, rushes and grasses dominate. These narrow-leaved emergent plants are wind pollinated and so lack the vivid flowers and scent required by insect pollinated plants.

Rushes are generally very thin with spiky tips. The soft rush has a very soft pith inside which closely resembles foam. Historically large quantities of soft rush were harvested, the pith being used for wicks in candles. Today the tough outer casing is sometimes used for basket making.

Sedges are easily recognised by the characteristic 'w' profile of their leaves. They occur in a huge variety of habitats and are a diverse group with around 80 species found in the British Isles. The river is dominated by two of the common species, greater pond sedge *(Carex riparia)* and lesser pond sedge *(Carex acutiformis)*.

Grasses are incredibly successful and have colonised just about every habitat. The main species that are found along the Pang are reed sweet grass *(Glyceria maxima)*, reed canary grass *(Phalaris arundinacea)* and common reed

(Phragmites australis). Pulling a leaf from the stem easily identifies the common reed. At the base it has a row of stout hairs, whereas the other two species have a paper like membranous collar. Reed sweet grass has a distinctive tip shape, like a ship's bow, unlike the flat tip of reed canary grass.

Reedmace

Reeds, sedges and grasses all provide excellent habitat for wildlife along the margins of the river. Small mammals such as water vole will use the cover, whilst the adult life stages of many aquatic insects will rest on the stems. Additionally many of these plant species do an excellent job of binding the soil and so help to prevent erosion along the banks. Fencing the river from excessive grazing and poaching by cattle helps promote this important marginal fringe.

Other narrow-leaved emergent plants recorded along the river include branched bur-reed *(Sparganium erectum)*

Flag iris

and greater reedmace *(Typha latifolia)*. Both these species thrive in slower areas such as backwaters with a good layer of silt and mud. Smaller broad-leafed emergent plants include water forget-me-not *(Myosotis scorpioides)* which produces delicate blue flowers for much of the year. Water mint *(Mentha aquatica)* and water-cress *(Rorippa nasturtium-aquaticum)* can also be commonly found. A larger broad-leaved aquatic plant that can occasionally be found along the Pang is the river water-dropwort *(Oenanthe fluviatilis)*, a species associated with clear, calcareous streams and rivers. It avoids deep silts, preferring to root in sands and gravel. This species has suffered a gradual decline over the last century due to increasingly nutrient rich water, river dredging and boat traffic. For this reason it has disappeared from the River Thames in Berkshire.

Where riffles are present, stream water-crowfoot *(Ranunculus penicillatus* subsp. *pseudofluitans)* often occurs. This plant is typical of good quality

Water crowsfoot   *Water dropwort*   *Water forgetmenot*

chalkstream habitats which have not been overdredged. It often grows into large beds of flowing fronds. In the summer, water-crowfoot grows to the surface of the river and produces a mass of brilliant white flowers. The plant belongs to the same family as buttercups with similar flower structure, yellow anthers surrounded by a ring of white petals. Water-crowfoot provides excellent habitat for a range of animals. Trout and grayling use the plant for cover whilst invertebrates attach themselves to the fronds catching food flowing past in suspension. It is for this reason that many river keepers and managers encourage its growth and plant water-crowfoot in areas where it is absent. It is unknown whether water-crowfoot reproduces by seed or through the spread of vegetative fragments but it is thought that the spread by seed may be rare.

The invertebrates. The River Pang has a very diverse invertebrate fauna, which is a reflection of its variation in physical habitat, comparing favourably with any river within the Thames catchment. Over the years, nearly 80 families of macroinvertebrates have been recorded in the river. Since 2000, 30 different species of caddisfly alone have been identified.

Along with common species, a number of uncommon and rare species have also been discovered. Perhaps the rarest invertebrate is the Thames ramshorn snail *(Gyraulus acronicus)*, which is now only found in three rivers in the whole country; the Pang, Windrush and Evenlode. It was once abundant throughout the Thames valley, hence its name. Today it resides in quiet reedy fringes away from fast flows, grazing the algae that grow on plants.

Another rarity, which is found on the bed of the river, is the tiny fine-lined pea mussel *(Pisidium tenuilineatum)*. A full-grown adult is no more than a few millimetres across and filters microscopic food particles from the water.

Kingcups   *Brooklime*

Recent surveys have shown that this species is more common in the Thames valley than previously thought. However, it is absent from large parts of Britain and the Pang has one of the strongest populations.

The lower sections of the river, as it approaches the Thames, have a small breeding population of club-tailed dragonfly *(Gomphus vulgattissimus)*. These impressive insects are restricted to only a handful of rivers in Southern England and Wales. As the name suggests they have a marked thickening of their tail and the female has a distinctive narrow yellow stripe along the abdomen. They breed in moderate to slow flowing stretches with a good layer of silt into which the larvae can burrow. The larvae live in the silt for between 3 and 5 years before emerging in May. In contrast to many other dragonflies, the club-tailed dragonfly prefers a degree of tree cover along the banks. This tree cover is vital for roosting adults and allows them to occur in good numbers where no emergent vegetation exists. The best time to see the adults on the wing is from early May to the end of June.

A number of the smaller, more slender damselflies can be found along the Pang. One of the most common is the banded demoiselle *(Calopteryx splendens)*. This stunning damselfly, one of the largest in Britain, will often be seen fluttering, butterfly-like, along thickly vegetated margins of the river. The males have a metallic green-blue body and distinctive dark blue bands on their wings. Males will often be seen chasing the green females. In areas of high population density fights between males are common to establish territories and claim the best perch sites. Successful males will closely guard the female as she lays her eggs, which can be on a wide variety of aquatic plants. By trapping air between their wings they are able to submerge themselves completely to lay their eggs safely directly into plant material. After 14 days the larvae hatch and live among submerged vegetation in the slower margins of the river. Development of the larva usually takes two years after which they emerge between mid-May and September.

Another damselfly found in similar habitat is the white-legged damselfly *(Platycnemis pennipes)*. This species has a more local distribution than the banded

Ephemera danica
with acknowledgements to Ben McFarland

demoiselle, being restricted to southern England, although there are signs that it is moving north, perhaps an indication of global warming. The Pang supports a good population although their lighter coloration makes them less obvious than many other species. They have distinctive dangling legs whilst in flight, with long feather like hairs. The white-legged damselfly is the only non-demoiselle damselfly with a courtship display. This consists of the female flying in short vertical movements and the males dangling their legs in front of their prospective mate.

The invertebrates that live in the faster flowing gravel areas typical of chalk streams have a number of strategies to cope with the currents they experience. Many animals flatten their body as a morphological adaptation to swift flow. Examples among the mayfly are Heptageniidae, which have wide flat heads and flattened legs and torso.

Of the twelve species of mayfly recorded from the Pang, the commonest are the *Baetis* species which are highly adapted to brisk currents. In slower flow they stand high on their legs and allow the current to swing them in the flow. They constantly adjust their body position to face the current and are capable of fast bursts of speed to avoid predation. In times of high flow they crouch down low between the gravels and are able to avoid the higher velocities.

Another common insect found in the swift flows of the Pang, are the riffle beetles. These tiny black beetles rely on their strong large clawed legs to grip the stony surface of the riverbed. Caddisflies, commonly known as sedge, have developed grapple hooks on their posterior prolegs, which form a very effective gripping mechanism. Additionally, the cased-caddisfly attaches its case to stones, weed and wood debris with silk whilst moulting. Some species of case-bearing caddisfly make their cases of large stones, which act as a ballast, pinning them to the substrate.

The black sedge *(Silo pallipes)* lives in the faster sections of the Pang and constructs its case with large stones along both sides. Its strong legs enable it to move around grazing algae despite the weight of the case and current. Such is the weight, if it loosens its grip, it slides off the stone and falls into sheltered 'dead water', rather than getting caught in the current. This reduces the risk of being eaten by fish. The black sedge can be host to a parasitic wasp *(Agriotyphus armatus)*. Amazingly this tiny wasp can

Thames Ramshorn with acknowledgements to Ben McFarland

swim down to the streambed, often in strong currents, and crawl along the riverbed to find a host.

As with other rivers, the invertebrate community that lives within the Pang plays a vital role in the functioning of the ecosystem. Along the river there are two dominant food sources that help support this diversity and each species living in the river is adapted to use these energy sources.

One source is the algae that grow on the surfaces of stones and larger plants. Scrapers and grazers including snails and many of the mayfly and caddisfly eat these algae. The other source comes from terrestrial vegetation in the form of leaves and twigs. Some species, such as the freshwater shrimp, *Gammarus pulex,* are shredders, using their jaws to break up leaves that have fallen into the water. Deposit and suspension feeders will then utilise the smaller pieces of food produced by the shredders and grazers. The larvae of the blackfly *(Simulium spp.)* cover rocks and other smooth surfaces with silk threads. They attach themselves to the silk with minute hooks around their posterior and 'stand' in the current using their fan-like mouthparts to catch tiny food particles in suspension.

A major potential threat to the invertebrate diversity of the Pang is the discovery of the American signal crayfish *(Pacifastacus leniusculus)* on the upper reaches of the river. This is a large crayfish which will eat most invertebrates it can catch. Currently its distribution along the river is restricted although it is likely to spread rapidly.

The nearby River Kennet has a major problem with signal crayfish and invertebrate sampling has indicated that the signal crayfish can virtually eliminate a number of species. The most vulnerable appear to be the larger, slow moving invertebrates such as some cased-caddisfly, leeches and ramshorn snails. The future of the Thames ramshorn snail is of particular concern. Many of the smaller fish such as the bullhead may also suffer either from direct predation or competition for food and space. It is likely that signal crayfish will eat the eggs of larger fish and therefore may affect the long-term population size of many fish species.

The fish. The Pang has an excellent diversity of fish species dominated, above Tidmarsh, by those species that enjoy the good water quality and the oxygen rich gravel substrate.

Brook lamprey
with acknowledgements to the Environment Agency

The species that are typically found along the river include our native brown trout, rainbow trout, grayling, chub, minnow, bullhead and stoneloach. These species spawn on the gravel and avoid the silty areas that would smother their eggs. They suffered badly during the low flows of the late 1980s, the early 1990s and the early 2000s. Many of

Stoneloach
with acknowledgements to the Environment Agency

the gravel areas used for spawning silted up and the slower flows resulted in warmer water with lower oxygen levels. This placed stress on many species, such as trout and grayling, which prefer the cool, clear, well oxygenated water so typical of chalk streams.

Despite the requirement for clean gravel and good flows, areas of slower flowing water are also essential for fry refuges. These areas, which can be backwaters or the margins of the river where plants and tree roots slow the flow, prevent fry and smaller species, such as minnow, from being washed away during times of high flow. During flood conditions fry will use the areas of slow flows in the floodplain as the river breaks its banks, only returning to the river channel as the floodwaters subside. In heavily engineered rivers, which have few backwaters and where the river is rarely in connection with its flood plain because of excessive dredging and flood embankments, the survival rates of fish are much lower than in a more natural river such as the Pang. Uncut banks of the Pang also enable thickly vegetated margins to develop, providing excellent hiding places from fish-eating predators.

One of the most abundant fish in the river is the tiny bullhead or miller's thumb *(Cottus gobio)*. Good water quality, coarse sediments and beds of submerged plants provide excellent habitat. In the chalk streams of southern England bullhead can grow rapidly, sometimes reaching a length of 60mm after their first year. They are a short-lived species rarely living beyond four years. This little fish is most active at night, emerging from beneath stones and large woody debris, to hunt invertebrates such as fly larvae and mayfly nymphs. Although they are abundant across southern England, the bullhead is rare throughout much of Europe.

Another small fish commonly found is the stickleback. Unlike the bullhead, this species thrives in a slower flowing habitat. Two species are found within the river. The three-spined stickleback lives in quiet areas of slow, open water; surrounded by areas of plants it can dart into to avoid predators. In contrast the nine-spined stickleback thrives in areas of very thick plant growth, stems or roots at the edges of the river. They can often be found in very shallow areas with a thick mat of leaves and low oxygen levels. The humble stickleback is perhaps best known for its breeding behaviour. The three-spined stickleback's creation of a nest of plant fragments on an open area of stream bed is unique. The male, using a special sticky secretion from the kidneys, constructs the nest in early spring. Once built he vigorously defends the nest from rival males, enticing a female with a zigzagging dance. When the female deposits her eggs in the nest the male takes over looking after the eggs and the newly born fry. He stays with them for a couple of weeks before leaving them to fend for themselves.

The beautiful grayling, 'the lady of the stream', has a fairly restricted distribution within Britain. Luckily a small yet stable population is found within the Pang. The characteristic large dorsal fin easily identifies the grayling from fish of similar habitats, such as trout. The male uses this dorsal fin to help clasp the female during spawning. Grayling feed throughout the water column, taking molluscs, worms and leeches on the bottom, invertebrates drifting through the water and food on the surface. Despite their adaptability in the range of food they eat, their distribution has declined dramatically throughout Europe, largely as a result of pollution. They are very sensitive to poor water quality and so only survive in the cleanest water, such as the Pang.

The lower reaches of the Pang are dominated by coarse fish such as roach, chub, perch and pike. The pike is perhaps the most notorious of all freshwater fish. It is an effective predator and can grow to a huge size in certain habitats. On a small river such as the Pang a fish of 10lbs would be considered a big fish. When first born, pike fry immediately start eating small invertebrates. They are also highly cannibalistic throughout their life. By the end of their first year they begin to eat other fish. The bulk of their diet consists of shoaling species such as roach, dace, minnow and trout. The pike, despite their occasional bad press, play a vital role in the functioning of a healthy ecosystem. They help to keep the numbers of other species at natural levels and help to 'weed out' weaker individuals.

Pike
with acknowledgements to the Environment Agency

The amphibians & reptiles. The majority of amphibian species are found in larger numbers in ponds and are not usually associated with rivers. However, the common frog can be found in some

Bullhead and eggs
with acknowledgements to the Environment Agency

locations such as slow, well-vegetated margins and backwaters. Here they may lay clumps of spawn in shallow warm water about 10cm in depth. Much of their life is spent in bank-side habitats, wet floodplain grassland or areas of damp open scrub and woodland. During the winter months they often use piles of dead wood as hibernation sites.

The most aquatic of reptiles, the grass snake, is an excellent swimmer, hunting frogs, invertebrates and small mammals. They are most likely to be encountered from mid-March to mid-May when they spend considerable time basking to raise their body temperature. They may be observed hunting the slower-flowing margins of the river later in the year. Eggs are laid in heaps of decaying vegetation left after floods and they also readily make use of compost heaps.

The mammals. A number of mammals rely on the river to survive. The water vole has decreased in many parts of Britain in recent years and is now the most rapidly declining mammal in Britain. This is mainly a result of habitat loss and predation by mink. There is evidence that the colonies along the Pang are declining and that the greatest danger comes from the mink.

Mink are native to North America, but have become established in much of the Thames valley. Many mink populations originated with escapees from fur farms. They are good swimmers and are sometimes mistaken for otters although they are considerably smaller and are in fact very similar to ferret in size. Our native water vole has little defence against these formidable predators

Mink

due to the mink's ability to both dive and enter the water vole's burrows. Action is being taken and many landowners are now trapping mink along the river.

Throughout most of the year water voles are active day and night, usually for about 2-4 hours at a time and their travels along the bank create runways in dense vegetation. During the winter months they stay in their burrows and their activity is greatly reduced, although they do not hibernate. Male water voles have a home range of approximately 130 metres, which can include a number of females. Each female's home range will consist of a number of entrances both above and below the waterline. Nests are normally underground within a complex labyrinth of

Water Vole
with acknowledgements to
the Environment Agency

burrows, although they will construct nests in dense tussocks of vegetation. They prefer steep banks normally over a metre high with good plant cover, which provide ideal burrowing conditions above normal water levels. Water voles are vegetarians and have a voracious appetite, capable of eating 80% of their body weight each day. During most of the year they eat mainly reeds, rushes and grass whereas in winter they rely on roots and rhizomes below the ground.

Another species of mammal that is closely associated with aquatic habitats is the water shrew. This tiny mammal likes fast flowing, unpolluted, clear rivers. Water shrews are likely to be found in many stretches along the Pang, although more research is needed into this overlooked species. It likes good plant cover, especially watercress and is mainly nocturnal. It dives to depths

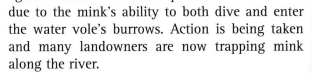

of 75cm to catch its prey of small invertebrates, such as *Gammarus* shrimp or caddisfly larvae. Like water voles, water shrews have extensive tunnel systems along the riverbank both above and below the waterline.

Currently it is thought that the otter, our largest freshwater predator, is absent from the Pang, but it is recovering nationally and spreading within the Thames catchment. The return of the otter to the Pang would be powerful testimony to the health of the river, as top predators are dependant on the whole ecosystem which supports them.

As we have seen, the Pang is a very special river. The river's chalk stream characteristics, with its stable flows and temperature, support an abundance of plant and animal species, making this river of important nature conservation interest.

Sources and further reading

Beebee T & Griffith R	*Amphibians and Reptiles* Collins 2000
Chinery M	*Collins Field Guide Insects of Britain* Harper Collins 1993
Croft P	*A key to major groups of British freshwater Invertebrates* Field StudiesCouncil
Fitter R & Manual	*Lakes, rivers, streams & ponds of Britain & NW Europe* Harper Collins 1994
Giles N	*Freshwater fish of the British isles: A guide for anglers and naturalists* Blackwell Science 1996
Greenaway D & Ward D	*In the Valley of the Pang* Privately published 2002
Greenhalgh M & Ovende D	*Collins pocket guide Freshwater Life* Collins 2007
Harris G & Corbet S	*Handbook of British mammals* Blackwell Science 1996
Mabey R	*Flora Britannica* Chatto & Windus 1997
Macan T	*A guide to freshwater animals* Longman 1959
Phillips R	*Wild Flowers of Britain* Pan Books 1997

CHAPTER NINE

Bricks, Iron and Boundaries
Exploring the parishes of Frilsham and Bucklebury

"The Pot Kiln"
9.7.07

Brick & Tile Making. Baked clay roof tiles are known to have been used in Greece in the 2nd millennium BC, but at that date bricks were only sun dried clay blocks. The Romans used hard fired clay bricks for building in Britain but the Saxons preferred wood for building and brick making died out in Britain.

Building with brick was only reintroduced from the Continent after the Norman Conquest and then only with imported bricks. Bricks were imported from Flanders as ballast in ships returning to East Coast ports having carried wool to the Continent. Brick making is known at Hull in the early 1300's. The first English bricks were 12" (0.3m) long and known as Great Bricks. These continued to be made until about 1500 and have been found in Pyt House near Ashampstead. The size of 9"x4½"x2¼" was fixed by law in 1571 and bricks of this size were known as Statute Bricks.

Bricks are not made of pure clay. Brick earth is a loam containing clay, sands and other minerals and it is these minerals, together with the amount of oxygen available during firing, which give them their colours. Iron rich brick earth and plentiful oxygen make bright red bricks, grey bricks result from low oxygen levels.

The Swanmore Series soils around Frilsham and Yattendon have been used for brick making since at least the 17th century. The will of John Pocock, brick burner of Frilsham, who died in 1664 is in the Berkshire Record Office and the Yattendon Kiln was advertising in the *Reading Mercury* in 1785.

Cat tracks

Bricks for large projects were dug and made on site by itinerant brick makers and the quarry pit often became a pond. Alfred Waterhouse advertised for brick makers to make bricks on site for the original Yattendon Court in 1878.

Brick and tile making involves first digging the brick earth and cleaning it of stones in a pug mill. Any missing elements, such as sand and chalk, are added at this stage and the bricks and tiles are formed in wooden moulds. They

Dog tracks on a tile

are then stacked to dry under rough shelters. Animals sometimes ran over the wet bricks and footprints are common – especially on tiles.

Most early bricks were burnt in clamps, not in enclosed kilns. This resulted in high oxygen levels and red bricks. Bricks in the middle of the clamp were hottest and hardest and sometimes deformed. Those on the outside were softer, often so soft that they could only be used for interior walls. Parts of Alfred Waterhouse's Court had to be taken down and rebuilt after the first winter because the soft bricks had frosted and crumbled.

Scotch kilns were introduced to overcome this problem. They were simply a very thick brick wall built to contain the stack and retain the heat. There was a narrow loading door and one or more firing holes to allow the heat to be sustained. The top was left open.

Whether burnt in a clamp or a kiln, the dried blocks were stacked for firing with ducts between them filled with fuel – bracken, twigs, sticks etc. The faces exposed to the duct became very hot and the sands in the mixture vitrified to leave glazed surfaces, bricks in contact stayed cooler and matt, the stacking pressure dented the blocks and left ridges and all these marks can be seen on old bricks. The firing lasted as long as two or three days and at night lit the sky brightly. It is probable that Burnt Hill near Yattendon got

Glazed surfaces and duct marks

its name from the glow in the sky when the local clamps were being fired. The blackout regulations introduced in 1939, at the start of World War 2, forced the industry to close since the bright lights would have provided a useful navigation marker for enemy bombers.

Iron foundries. Iron making in Britain started in about 700BC but it had been practised on the Continent long before this. At first tiny quantities of iron were made using iron ores found on or near the surface, melted with locally produced charcoal. Slag from the operation has been found in woods in the Chilterns, but the main centres of production in Southern Britain were the Forest of Dean and the Weald of Kent.

Iron rapidly replaced bronze for the production of tools and weapons. Early furnaces produced *wrought iron* in small blooms which contained a mixture of pure iron and slag. The slag had to be driven out by heating and hammering the bloom to make a small billet of iron. The billets were then used by blacksmiths to forge implements, tools, weapons etc. This was a slow process and ensured that iron objects remained costly. It has been estimated that a Roman furnace would produce about 100kg of iron in 24 hours. Forging a single Roman sword might take another 7 hours with an additional 30 hours to finish it. Improved furnaces made possible the separation of the slag within the furnace thus allowing the iron to be poured into a mould. This was *cast iron*. It was harder but more brittle than wrought iron.

Local foundries developed from blacksmiths' shops to provide iron objects for the community. The 18th century agricultural revolution provided the stimulus to make improved ploughs etc and foundries blossomed. They made ploughs, tools, nails and domestic items. Their account books show that they also repaired metal objects. These were usually large items such as ploughs, but they also repaired trivial items which must have been uneconomic and done as a favour for a neighbour.

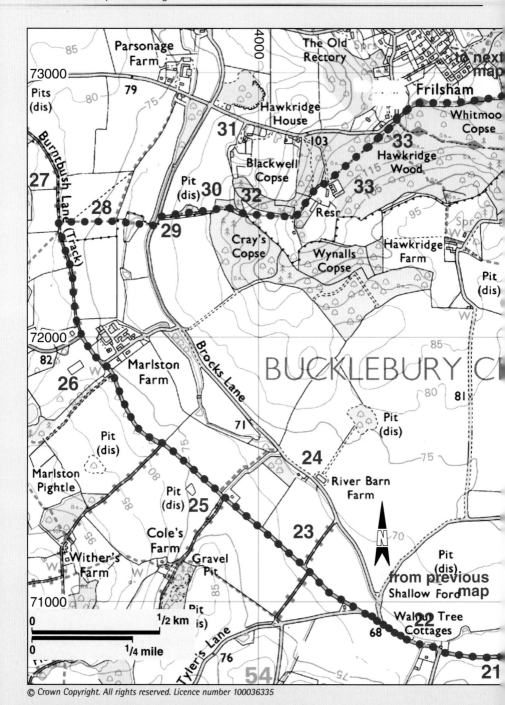

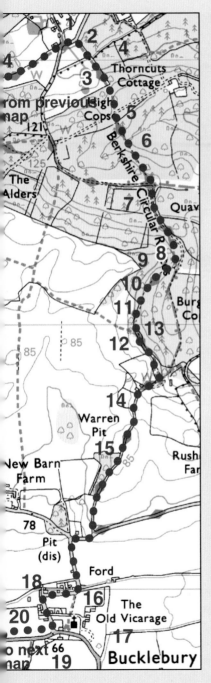

This walk includes parts of Frilsham and Bucklebury parishes. It starts and finishes at the 'Pot Kiln'

- **It is about 5 miles or 8 km long. The route is along wide, clear and well marked tracks.**
- **There are two modest hills and surfaces can be uneven and muddy.**
- **There are eight stiles**
- **There are about 1¾ miles (3km) of road walking.**
- **Horses and riders may be encountered.**

Ordnance Survey map Explorer 158 'Newbury and Hungerford' will be useful.

Frilsham is mentioned in Domesday Book. The place name means *Frithel's Village.* It had been a Saxon royal estate, and was probably based on a settlement near Frilsham church. **Soils.** Except for a narrow strip of alluvium along the river the whole walk is over *Frilsham and Swanmore* Series soils. Both these have a high clay content and provided good brick making material. Most of the large hollows around the Pot Kiln are the result of digging to supply the kiln.

1. The Pot Kiln pub. The Barr family made bricks here from at least the mid 19th century until World War 2 blackout regulations enforced closure. They would probably not have lasted much longer in face of competition from mass produced bricks. The enclosed *Scotch Kiln* stood just behind the pub.

2. Species rich hedge. Look for hawthorn, blackthorn, crab, field maple, cherry, ash, hazel, elder and holly. The hedge provides a valuable link for wildlife across the valley.

3. Saw & potash pits. Trees were often sawn into planks and beams on site. A pit about 6 feet (2m) deep, 10 feet (3m) long and 3 feet (1m) wide was dug and the trunk rolled onto beams laid across it. One sawyer stood on top of the trunk, another stood in the pit and they cut the tree lengthways with a two-handed pit saw. When refilled the pits have this distinctive shape. Waste wood, twigs, bracken and bramble were burned to a fine ash in a nearby pit to make *potash*. This was soaked in water which was then drawn off to make lye for soap making and washing. The residue was used as a flux and added to sand to make glass. Cheaper North American potash of better quality ended this practice about 1830.

Bricks drying at the Pot Kiln c1930.

4. Brick earth quarry. The large pit in this wood provided sandy clay for the brickworks.

5. Boundary bank. This substantial bank separated the area of fields from the wooded area. It may have been a more important boundary, perhaps of an estate.

6. Fields to copses. The first detailed map of this area (1761) shows most of the land used as fields bounded by hedges which by 1877 had become copses. The great demand for hazel and ash hurdles to protect the new hedges around newly enclosed Common Fields and along newly constructed Turnpike Roads made this the best use for poor quality land. The flora of the woods demonstrates their history. It is species poor, except along the old hedge lines where there are still patches of Ancient Woodland Indicator Species such as bluebell.

7. Ancient pond. This artificial circular pond was probably dug to water stock in the old fields and is therefore at least 150 years old.

8. Double tree. This beech has grown either from two saplings deliberately planted in the same hole or from two seeds – possibly in a squirrel's hoard.

9. Flower rich meadow. When the fields were converted to copses this small area seems to have been forgotten. The soil is very acid and acid soils do not usually support a rich flora, but over seventy species were counted on the first survey and others have been added since. It is private and permission must be obtained from Yattendon Estate for a visit.

10. Ancient road. Clearly defined by a substantial bank on either side, this road is shown in 1761 and led from Hawkridge and Bucklebury to the old fields. It runs along the edge of the heavy clay Swanmore soils – note the steep escarpment to the east and the sandy, gravelly soils in wind blown tree roots.

Ruins of a Scotch kiln by permission of Mr & Mrs Tiranti

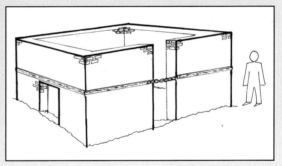

Sketch of a Scotch Kiln

11. Settlement. The 1761 map shows a settlement near here and a road leading west. The bank of this road lined with very ancient stools is still clearly visible.

12. Ancient oaks. The oak on the bank is 3.83m in girth giving a planting date of c.1720. The coppiced oak at the footpath junction has a girth of 4.05m giving an age of at least 340 years. It is probably much older and the girth has been repressed by cutting.

13. Possible potash pit. See Note 3 for an explanation.

14. Old Hawkridge. The house appears to be mainly 16th century but may be much older. It seems to be built on a Spring Line site where there was a reliable water supply. It was built using early local bricks. Note how uneven and irregular they are.

15. Warren Pit. This may be a swallow hole caused, or enlarged by, quarrying. Water running off the clays passes through the permeable Frilsham soils into the chalk aquifers beneath.

16. River Pang & Black Barn Mill (site). A mill is listed in Domesday Book and this channel may have been the artificial mill leat with the original channel by-passing it (possibly to the north). The small building down stream of the bridge contained a small modern mill.

17. Bucklebury. This is a very ancient settlement. It was certainly the headquarters of a major Saxon royal estate spreading from the south side of Bucklebury Common to the edge of Frilsham Common. It was later divided into four separate manors of which Bucklebury itself and Marlston were two. The name means *Burghild's Fort.* It may have been one of the fortified settlements established by King Alfred as a defence against the invading Danes or it may simply refer to a fortified manor house. *Burghild* is a woman's name.

18. Bucklebury foundry. This probably developed out of a local blacksmith's business. It was owned

Bucklebury Foundry water wheel

Bucklebury Church doorway

by the Hedges family from the early 1600's to 1904. A set of ledgers exists for the business covering the years 1736-1773. They give lists of customers' names and the work done for them. They show that the business made and repaired all kinds of farm equipment, domestic items and tools and that their customers lived as far away as Yattendon. They also shod horses. Some of the repairs were trivial and were probably done as a favour, such as *mending a cheese toaster 6d* (2½p). The next nearest foundry was Baker's at Compton.

19. Church. It is mentioned in 1070 and the earliest part is the Late Norman south door. The porch was built in 1663 and the gate was made at the foundry in 1827. The whole building was sensitively restored in 1911 and 1912. Pressure from The Society for the Protection of Ancient Buildings (founded by William Morris) prevented the insensitive restorations inflicted on many ancient churches in the Pang Valley.

20. The Victory Room & Playing Field. The village hall was bought from

Frilsham Football Club and erected to celebrate the end of World War I and to commemorate the 37 men of the parish who were killed. The hedge along the road side was cut and laid by The Pang Valley Conservation Volunteers.

21. Hedges. The road is shown lined with hedges in 1761, but the modern hedges are not particularly species rich. Look for hawthorn, blackthorn, hazel, dogwood, field maple, spindle.

22. Embanked channel. These embankments may be evidence that the modern channel is an artificial mill leat constructed to raise a head of water for a mill. The 1877 Ordnance Survey map shows two, possibly three, minor channels at this point and these may indicate the site of a mill.

23. Water meadows? The modern channel runs on the far side of a long, damp, low area in the field. This may indicate that the modern channel is the head channel for a water meadow although no sign of a water meadow system is shown on the 1877 map. However, there are extensive systems up stream and down stream of this site.

24. River Barn. A small watermill at this site drove chaff cutters, saws etc. for the farm. The wheel was made in the foundry in 1884.

25. Pit in field. Possibly for brick earth but probably for chalk. Chalk was spread thickly on the soil and ploughed in. It raised the soil pH to a level where wheat could grow. Frilsham soils are very acid and only rye will grow without liming.

Iron slag from a bloom

26. Marlston. One of the four sub-manors of the Saxon Bucklebury estate. In 1066 it was granted to the Monastery of Noyon in Normandy and later passed to the Prior of Sheen. In 1242 it belonged to Galfridus Martel and the place name comes from *Marteleston* which means *Martel's settlement.* The manor house was on the site of Brockhurst School which was itself built as a country house in 1895-9 for the Palmers of Reading. The church is a heavily rebuilt Norman church, the north door dating from c.1200.

27. Burnt Bush Lane. This was a major road in 1761.

28. Riverside. Note the owl box and the duck decoy pond. The channel along the roadside is artificially raised and served either to raise the head of water for the mill at River Barn or to flood the water meadows – or both.

Cast iron grave marker made at the foundry

29. Saxon boundary. The English Saxons of the 9th - 11th centuries were methodical and legalistic people far more civilised than most of their contemporaries. Land was transferred by written and witnessed charters which carefully described the boundaries of the land. This track with its double banks is a late 10th century boundary.

30. Quarry. This appears to be cutting through the Frilsham beds into the chalk.

31. Hawkridge House was built c.1890 by Mr Harry Weber who had made a fortune from mining in the Transvaal. In 1903 he provided the village well for Hampstead Norreys. He had a lavish lifestyle until his investments failed in 1907 and he had to sell up.

32. Laurel indicates acid soils.

33. Hawkridge Wood. In 956AD King Eadwig granted this wood to Abingdon Abbey. The charter boundary reads; *From the Paegan Burnan, th' to the Dic, th' a the Dic on thaene hagan ...*'From the River Pang, then to the dyke, then always by the dyke to the game enclosure ...' The walk runs up the dyke and the large bank at the top was the *hagan*. Other parts of the list describe flax fields and a wayside cross. In 1259 a woman was found dead in the wood. This has been woodland for over 1000 years, a fact confirmed by its rich flora and uneven land surface.

34. Sulhams Copse. Another Ancient Wood. Note the brick earth pits and the Veteran Oak on the bank. A girth of 5.03m makes it at least 350 years old.

Sources and further reading

Victoria County History – Berkshire

Morris J (Ed)	*Domesday Book – Berkshire*	Phillimore 1979
Ekwall E (ed)	*The Concise Dictionary of English Place-names*	OUP 1974
Mabey R	*Flora Britannica*	Chatto & Windus 1997
Williamson T	*Shaping Medieval Landscapes*	Windgather Press 2003
Greenaway D & Ward D (Eds)	*In the Valley of the Pang*	Privately published 2002
Rackham O	*The History of the Countryside*	Dent 1986
Natural England	*Ancient Woodland Vascular Plants.*	
Palmer F	*The Blacksmiths Ledgers*	1970
Humphreys AL	*Bucklebury*	Privately published 1932
Prizeman J	*Your House, the outside view*	1982
Sim D, Ridge I	*Iron for the Eagles*	Tempus Publishing 2002

CHAPTER TEN

Hill fort, ancient trees and green lanes
Grimsbury Castle and Bucklebury Common

On grimsbury castle

Hill Forts. Hill forts are a common feature of the chalk downlands and what we see dates from the Iron Age. Recent research has shown that many had Bronze Age predecessors.

Their function varied from being a defended town with a large population to a sparsely populated place of refuge. Danebury near Devizes is an example of the former while Grimsbury seems to have had few residents. They indicate a large, well organised community which could feed and support the large number people needed to create the massive banks and deep ditches. The militarised society of the period may have developed as a result of an expanding population putting pressure on resources. Certainly by 55BC Julius Caesar could report the country as densely settled with many cattle. He also encountered a warlike and mobile population which came near to defeating him.

The Origin of 'Greens'. Many 'greens' were founded by illegal settlers on manorial waste land and they are frequently found around the edges of large commons. A landless person would build a hut in an unfrequented spot or on the edge of a trackway and start cultivating a small patch of ground around it. He would be fined every year by the manor court and eventually the fine became a rent.

Sometimes Greens were more formally established as planned farmsteads designed to use the resources of the Common and an allocation of crofts and Open Field strips.

Drove Roads. Droving takes two forms. There is the local movement of animals from one farm to another or to market, and there is the long distance movement of animals from breeding areas to fattening areas. Both types of droving used the same lanes and tracks. Narrow lanes with high banks on either side allowed large numbers of animals to be driven by two or three men with dogs. The wider areas may have been resting places, and greens like Westrop may have been overnight harbouring sites.

Long distance droving involved larger groups of men. Cattle and sheep were driven from Wales to midland grazing areas and to market in London. There are records of drovers driving animals from Wales in the early 14th century. Animals were gathered from all over Scotland and driven south to fatten and then to supply the growing populations of England's towns. The drovers also performed a banking service and were frequently entrusted with carrying large sums of money.

It was not only animals that were driven. Turkeys and geese were driven to market. Geese had their feet coated with tar to prevent them wearing out their webs and going lame.

When the Welsh drovers reached their destination it was their practice to turn their dogs loose to find their own way home; the arrival of the dogs warned the families that the men were not far behind!

The coming of the railways ended long distance droving. However, the terrible agricultural depression of the late 19th and early 20th centuries meant that farmers were still sometimes forced to drive cattle rather than transport them by train.

Dating Ancient Trees. The ages of trees can be estimated by measuring their girth at about 1.5m above the ground and then applying the measurement to the dating curve below.

However, there are many *caveats!* A tree growing in the open, perhaps in a park, will not be competing for light nor for nutrients and will therefore grow faster than a tree growing on poor soil in a shady situation. Two trees with similar girths growing within a few hundred metres of each other can have greatly different ages if one is within a wood and one on the edge. The dating curve only supplies a very approximate date. To improve on the age derived from the curve one should use the formulae given in John White's paper which can be obtained via the Forestry Commissions website (see Sources).

Pollard, stub trees and *coppice stools* almost stop growing when their branches are cropped and so are smaller in girth for their age than an uncut *maiden* tree. Allow an extra 30% for these trees. Oliver Rackham provides a rule of thumb for aging old coppice stools. Work done in the 1970s when woods and hedges were being grubbed, indicated that the diameter of a coppice stool measured in feet could be used to <u>estimate</u> its age by allowing one foot for every hundred years. Thus a three foot diameter stool was probably about 300 years old. This applied to hazel, ash, oak and beech. Field maple grows a little faster and sweet chestnut much faster.

Very old trees are difficult to age. A complex calculation is available to do this. Again see John White's paper.

The curve provided below is for maiden oak trees. Other trees have different growth rates and the curve will not apply. However, beech and ash fit the curve up to about 150 years and it is unusual to find maiden trees of either species much older than about 200 years.

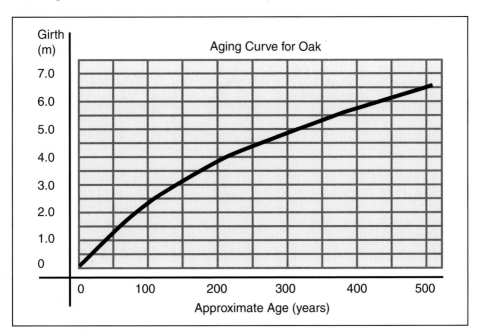

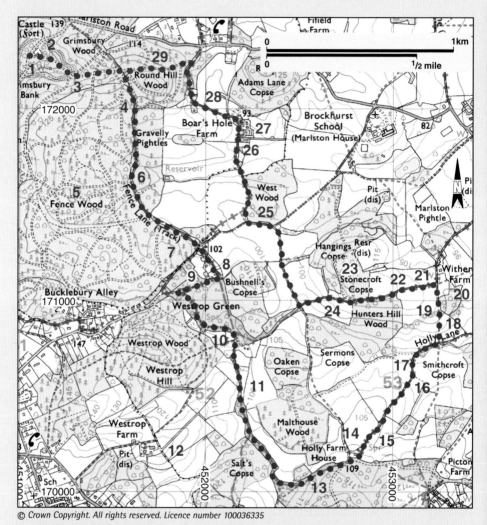

This walk includes Grimsbury Castle, Fence Lane and the edge of Bucklebury Common. It starts and finishes at Grimsbury Castle.

- It is about 5 miles or 8 km long. The route is along wide, clear and well marked tracks.
- There are several modest hills and surfaces can be uneven and muddy.
- Tractors and farm machinery use these trackways.
- Horses and riders may be encountered.

Ordnance Survey map Explorer 158 'Newbury and Hungerford' will be useful.

1. Grimsbury Castle. As with Grim's Ditch and Grim's Dyke, the Saxons credited the fort's creation to the gods since it was too massive for them to believe that men had built it. Grimsbury means *Grim's Fort* and Grim was a by-name of Woden. By-names were used when referring to gods because possession of a tribal god's real name was thought to give power to their enemies. The fort is perched on the watershed between the Pang and Kennet valleys. It is an Early Iron Age hill fort. Small excavations were carried out 1957 & 1960. Very little dating evidence or signs of habitation were found and this may mean that the fort was a refuge rather than a settlement. Some forts show signs of planned streets and house plots. At Grimsbury the entrances are on the west, north and north east. The western side is protected by an outer north-south bank. The shallow pit near the map board is probably a 19th century pit for making wood ash. Wood ash was soaked in water to make lye for washing liquid. The

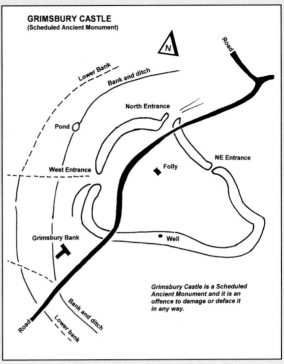

With acknowledgements to English Heritage and Newbury Museum

Grimsbury Castle

*A bundle planted beech
near the east gate*

Grimsbury Folly

residue was used as a flux to lower the temperature at which sand melted when making glass. The well in the southern bank is not likely to be contemporary with the fort. The long mound north of it is a 'pillow mound' – a medieval artificial rabbit warren.

Note the bundle planted beech near the east entrance.

2. The Folly. This was built in the 18th century and is a private house.

3. The Woods. These are a recent feature. When the fort was constructed the land was open and probably cultivated. In 1761 the area was open heath land. Although there are bluebells in parts of the fort interior they have not yet spread back over the defences and appear to be absent from most of the surrounding woods. Oak has been replanted in Round Hill Wood but beech will not be replanted because it is thought that global warming will make the future climate unsuitable.

4. Fence Lane. This is a very ancient route. It is continued to the NNW by Old Street. Together the lanes link the Ridgeway with Bucklebury Common and the Kennet Valley. It was probably in existence through woods before the fort was built and before the land was cleared and cultivated. This is indicated by the bluebells on the large banks which line the

Fence Lane

lane. The wood name 'Gravelly Pightles' shows that it was originally a field. 'Pightle' means a field cleared from woodland. The large banks were built to keep stock from breaking into the woods and copses as they were driven along the lane. Copses were especially valuable. The large oak and beech trees and stools indicate the minimum age of the banks.

5. Fence Wood. This wood contains a good range of Ancient Woodland Indicator Species (AWIS) and was probably not a field.

6. Gravel pit. This is a gravel quarry for road materials. The gravel was probably hauled out on a rope-way since there is no obvious access ramp.

Ancient oak pollard at Point 9

7. Conifer plantation. These dense plantations extinguish original ground flora. The Forestry Commission is trying to remove those planted in ancient woods and sometimes original plants re-appear from seeds dormant in the soil when this is done.

8. Westrop Green. In 1761 this was called *'Westip Green'*. Westrop Cottage was a pub and there is a pond beside the track. This may have been a stopping place for drovers providing drink for man and beast.

9. Pollard Oak. This is 4.6 metres in girth and is probably about 400 years old. Pollards were created by cutting young trees about 3 metres above the ground where the re-growth was above the reach of cattle. The re-growth was then cropped for timber and fire-wood at regular intervals.

Ancient oak stub at Point 10

10. Oak Stub. Stubs were created in the same way as pollards but seem to have been used as boundary markers. Note the scarring caused by centuries of cropping. With a girth of 5.85 metres, this tree is probably about 600 years old.

11. Ancient Landscape. This is definitely an ancient area. Note the scattered settlement, the small irregular fields and woods. The banks have a rich flora. Look for – wood mellick, enchanter's nightshade, yellow pimpernel, gooseberry, stichwort, herb Robert, bluebell, violet, sanicle, pignut, primrose, celandine, strawberry and the old field maple, oak and ash stools

12. Westrop Farm. From the Old English *'West thorp'* meaning *'the outlying dairy farm to the west of the manor.'*

13. Holly Wood. Holly was grown and cut for winter fodder for stock and deer. Note the large bank and ditch.

14. Holly Farm House. Built c.1850 on an older site. Shown in 1761. Note the stock watering pond in the wood edge.

15. Holly Lane. This is undoubtedly an ancient lane and is mapped in 1761. The hedges are species rich. Look for: field maple, hawthorn and blackthorn, wild plum, hazel, holly, elder, sallow and dogwood.

16. Sunken Lane. Caused by rain water washing away soil loosened by feet, hooves and wheels over many centuries. The hedges are equally rich in shrubs and ground flora. Look in the hedge bottom for, wood mellick, primrose, bluebell, dog's mercury, enchanter's nightshade, greater stitchwort and wood speedwell.

17. Ancient Woodland. The lane runs along a terrace in the steep valley side and was once hedged. The crooked ash trees were caused by layering and the terrace was caused by traffic loosening the soil and moving it downhill.

18. Re-sown Grassland. Note: red and white clover, dandelion, hawkweed, mayweed, thistle, ragwort and black medick.

19. Strip of Ancient Woodland. Look for bluebell, wood mellick, enchanter's nightshade, dog's mercury etc.

20. Pheasant Release Pen. Without organised shooting it is likely that many ancient coppices would have been grubbed out and put to other uses.

21. Species Rich Hedge. The maiden oak has a girth of 4.2m and is about 250 years old. In the hedge I counted six species – blackthorn, field maple, hawthorn, dogwood, hazel, ash

22. Ancient Pollard Oak. This tree has a girth of 4.95 metres and is probably at least 350 years old. Look for badger dung pits; badgers use their latrines to mark clan territory boundaries.

23. Stonecroft Copse. The element 'croft' indicates that it was once an individually owned paddock. 'Copse' means that it was planted (with hazel) as a coppice, but this is not supported by the ground flora. There are plenty of bluebells. Perhaps it was 'the copse near the stony paddock'.

24. Hedge with Pollard Willows. It is unusual to find willow pollards in a

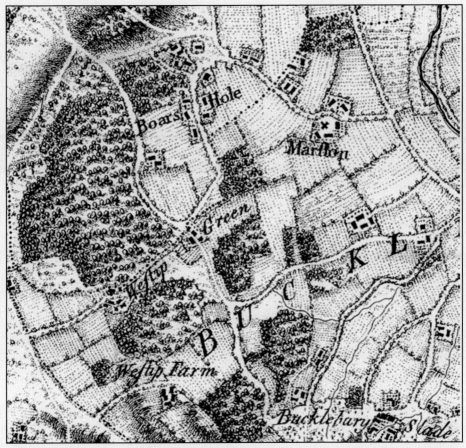

The area in 1761. Note how little it has changed.

hedge intended to be stock proof since they create a weak area.

25. West Wood. The rhododendrons are pretty but highly invasive and very destructive of the natural ground flora.

26. Quarry and view to Brockhurst School. The name means *'Badger Heath.'* Originally Marlston House, it was built in 1895-9 by Edward Burgess for Mr George William Palmer (of Huntley & Palmer) on the site of an older house. In 1761 it was called *'Marston'.* The tall chimney was part of a steam driven pump which drew water from an 24m (80ft) well and pumped it to a reservoir on Adams Lane Copse Hill whence it was piped around the estate. The pump house also housed the estate laundry. It is now a private house.

27. Boars Hole Farm. Appears on maps of 1761. In 1877 it was Borough Hall Farm. I have been unable to find any earlier references. There are a number of swallow holes on the farm, perhaps these were noted wallows when wild boar still roamed the woods. Note the 'Model Farm' layout and somewhat incongruous 'railway' sheds. On the north side there is a newly restored granary . Granaries were used to store seeds and animal food. It is built on staddle stones; these stone mushrooms were intended to stop rats and mice climbing into the granary. They also lifted the floor off the ground and allowed air to circulate thus keeping the granary and its contents dry.

28. Dead Oaks. These trees have been killed by trampling and by cultivation over their roots. Cattle and machinery should be kept at least 10m away from tree boles.

29. Round Hill Wood. This is an old hazel coppice with oak standards. It has been coniferised with larches. Larch drops its needles in winter and thus lets in more springtime light and this allows more of the ground flora to survive.

Sources and further reading

Victoria County History – Berkshire

Morris J (Ed)	*Domesday Book – Berkshire*	Phillimore 1979
Ekwall E (Ed)	*The Concise Dictionary of English Place-names*	OUP 1974
Mabey R	*Flora Britannica*	Chatto & Windus 1997
Williamson T	*Shaping Medieval Landscapes*	Windgather Press 2003
Rackham O	*The History of the Countryside*	Dent 1986
Rackham O	*Woodlands*	Harper Collins 2006
Toulson S	*The Drovers*	Shire Publications 2005
Godwin F and Toulson S	*The Drovers Roads of Wales*	Wildwood House 1977
Taylor C	*Roads and Tracks of Britain*	Dent 1979
White J	*Estimating the Age of Large and Veteran Trees in Britain* Forestry Commission 1998	

(www.forestry.gov.uk/publications/information note/estimating the age of large and veteran trees in britain)

CHAPTER ELEVEN

A stroll around Bucklebury Common
Exploring the central part of the Common

Bucklebury
Fishponds 30.4.07

Bucklebury Common. This is an important area of lowland acid heath. It is underlain by a sheet of gravels deposited by an ancient river braid during one of the earlier cold periods possibly about half a million years ago. The ancestors of the Pang and Kennet have cut down on either side of it leaving the Common as a suspended river terrace. The gravels are covered by acid heath soils from which the nutrients have been leached downwards by rain to form an acid and infertile *podzol* with an underlying iron pan.

In the millennia after the last Ice Age it may have been covered with a thin layer of more fertile soils and trees and, like many other heath lands, been reduced to a heath by the poor farming techniques of early farmers.

The Common provided grazing for the commoners of the manor of Bucklebury for many hundreds of years and probably served Roman, Iron Age and Bronze Age farmers in the same way. The right to graze animals was attached to particular properties within the manor. A tenant with common rights could graze one horse or cow for every acre he held in the Open Fields.

Bucklebury manor was held by Reading Abbey from the early 12th century until 1540. It then passed into the ownership of John Winchcombe, son of 'Jack of Newbury'. During the Second Battle of Newbury in October 1644, part of the Parliamentary Army camped on the Common before attacking the king at Shaw House.

In 1834 the Lord of the Manor proposed the formal enclosure of the Common. The proposal was fought by a remarkable Methodist lay preacher named John Morton. He took the fight to the House of Commons and won.

During World War 2 extensive areas of the Common were used to stockpile military equipment. The soil was scraped away into large mounds to reveal the dry gravel surface.

The Meaning of 'Common'. This has already been discussed in Chapter Six in the context of Ashampstead Common. However, it is worth repeating before discussing commons in more detail. All Commons belong to some person or to some organisation. They differ from ordinary land in that people other than the owner have defined rights over them. These people are titled Commoners and the Common Rights are usually linked to a farm or a house. The rest of the population has no rights to access the common or to exploit its resources other than those specifically granted by the owner. For example, a Commoner may have the Rights to graze animals and to take firewood and these Rights are enshrined in Common Law and cannot be removed by the owner. However, the owner could deny them to non-Commoners, but might grant the right to play cricket or to exercise dogs. These Rights are simple privileges and can be revoked at any time.

The Origins of Commons and their Use. In the Early Medieval Period (before about 1000AD) populations were small and land plentiful. The land had been divided into Estates for several thousand years and consisted of arable and grazing land surrounded by extensive woods and heaths. These areas became known as Manorial Waste and they were used as wood pasture where animals could both graze on herbage and browse on foliage. 'Waste' did not have the modern meaning of 'rubbish'. The waste was a vital resource and it was used to graze animals, to supply timber and firewood and bedding for stalled animals. The animals grazing on the waste by day and penned or stalled by night transferred nutrients in their dung to the arable. As populations grew arable land expanded and more animals grazed the Waste until the danger of over exploitation was recognised, but not before some manors had ploughed every inch of their land.

In 1235 major landowners prevailed on the king to issue a statute, the Statute of Merton, which allowed them to enclose pasture land, including

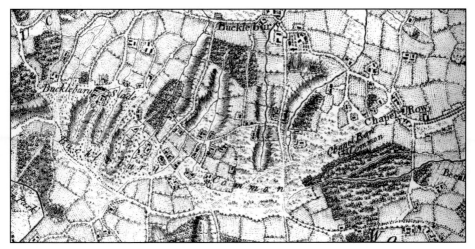

Bucklebury Common in 1761

wood pasture, as long as they left each tenant enough to run his holding efficiently and as long as the enclosure did not block a tenant's access to his land. As a result of this there was a considerable amount of enclosure of what had been common land, to create deer parks, private woods and coppices which were then preserved and managed intensively. A case which may have been designed to test the statute was brought to court in Reading in 1240. The prior of Poughly Abbey, near Chaddleworth in West Berkshire, claimed that the lord of the manor of Bradfield had prevented him from exercising his right of common pasture in a wood in Ashampstead parish by building a fence around the wood. The court found against him.

Commons were defined and carefully protected. Their boundaries were formally inspected in the same way that parish boundaries were 'beaten' on Rogation Sunday and encroachments were noted and remedied. An enclosed paddock called a *pound* was maintained, in which illegally grazing animals could be impounded, until their owner redeemed them by payment of a fine. Sensible by-laws were imposed by Manor Courts to prevent over exploitation of commons. For example, a commoner might only be allowed to graze animals in summer if he had enough enclosed land on which to graze them over the winter. Often this number was fixed for a particular farm. This is the case with Bucklebury properties to which Common Rights are attached. The allowance is included in their title deeds and sometimes marked on a plaque attached to the house. Another example might require a commoner only to remove firewood or furze on his back, not in a cart. Each common had its own rules enforced by the Manor Court.

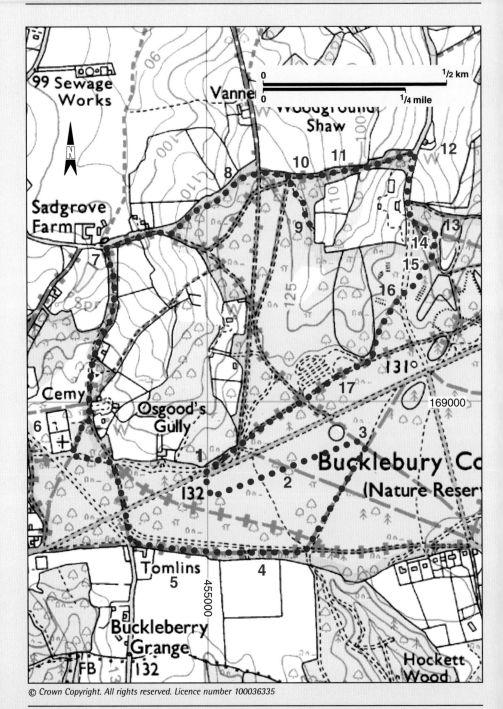

This walk circles part of Bucklebury Common close to the east of Upper Bucklebury village. It starts and finishes at Angels Corner.

- It is about 2½ miles or 4 km long. Most of the route is along wide, clear and well marked tracks, but the multitude of paths on the Common can cause confusion. A compass will be useful to help in establishing correct paths.
- There are several modest hills on this walk and surfaces can be uneven and muddy.
- Horses and riders and mountain bikers may be encountered.

Ordnance Survey map Explorer 158 'Newbury and Hungerford' will be useful.

1. Angels Corner. The name is recorded in 1699 but there is no clue to its origin. Perhaps it got its name during the period of religious miracles reported between 1158 and 1165 when a plague affecting men and beasts in Bucklebury was halted by the Abbot of Reading Abbey. He sprinkled water in which the reliquary containing the hand of St James had been dipped and the plague stopped. A second miracle involved oxen which, while being used to transport materials for a cross to mark the sprinkling spot, moved unguided to the site.

2. Conservation Area. This is one of several areas which the Bucklebury Heathland Conservation Group have created and now maintain. Look for: ling, cross leaved heath, bell heather and the grey lichen *cladonia portentosa* which contains the antibiotic usnic acid.

The Bucklebury Heathland Conservation Group. This was formed in 1992 by a group of people concerned by the disappearance of the special heathland, the result of centuries of grazing, under a dense mass of birch and Scots pine. By cutting and stump killing they have been able to recover areas of the old heathland vegetation (of ling,

Bucklebury Common c 1928
with acknowledgements to Christine Storey

cross-leaved heath, gorse etc.), with its attendant birds and animals. They work to a programme which is published on the website of the Friends of the Pang, Kennet and Lambourn Valleys (www.pangandkennetvalleys.org.uk). New helpers are always welcome!

Navigation tip! Walk with the sound of the road on your left!

3. Topsoil mounds. There are three of these mounds. They are formed from the soil scraped away during World War 2 to leave a dry gravel surface on which to store military equipment. Note the lushness of the bracken in contrast with the cleared area.

4. Oak and bank. This is probably a 'stub' used as a boundary marker. Its girth is 4.45m. This indicates a minimum age of about 450 years. Note the ditch is inside the bank. It is therefore to keep animals from escaping from the Common on to the cultivated land. The field outside the boundary is Hockets Field which was given to the parish in 1937.

5. Tomlin's. This is a Common Edge settlement from which both the resources of the Common and the enclosed fields could be exploited. The numerous 'Greens' around the edge of the Common served the same purpose for the poorer people. In 1902 the parish had a bonfire here as part of the celebrations of King Edward VII's coronation. See also the Coronation Oak note 9.

Ancient oak stub on the southern boundary bank

6. Cemetery. The wall was necessary to keep grazing animals out. Note the cast iron grave markers. These were made in Bucklebury foundry.

7. Sadgrove Farm. This is another typical 'Common Edge Settlement'.

8. Boundary & holloway. This sunken road has been carved out by centuries of wear. Note the richer ground flora in this area which indicates that it has a long history as a wood.

Cast iron grave marker made at the foundry

The Coronation Oak

Nuttage gate
with acknowledgements to Christine Storey

9. Coronation Oak. One of several ancient pollard oaks in this area. Surprisingly it is a sessile oak and ancient sessile oaks are unusual in Pang Valley woods, unless they have been planted for timber. They are usually found in the west of the country. Perhaps the acorn from which this one grew found its way from Wales to Bucklebury in a drover's pocket. Its girth is 7.2m which indicates a minimum age of 500 years. However, as with the stub oak (Note 4) the regular cutting will have slowed its growth and it could be 650 years old.

In 1902, 1200 people picnicked around the tree to celebrate the coronation of Edward VII.

10. View into a Deer Park. This is part of Bucklebury Farm Park. It was set up in 1992 and holds red deer, fallow deer, Japanese sika deer and axis deer, also known as Japanese spotted deer.

11. Coppice. Not all the Common was open and grazed. It also provided timber and poles and oak bark for tanning. This area is a very old hazel coppice with oak standards. The very ancient oak has a girth of 5.17m indicating an age of about 350 to 400 years. Note the rich flora. Look for: herb Robert, yellow pimpernel, enchanter's nightshade, woundwort, celandine, bluebell, wood sorrel ....

12. Nuttage Gate. This means 'place where nuts grow' and may refer to the nearby hazel coppice. It was one of the many gates across roads leading into the Common.

13. Fish Ponds. These two were built by Reading Abbey in the 12th century. There were another three in the grounds of the manor house. They were used to supply fish to the abbey for use during fast days when meat could not be eaten. Nowadays the fishing rights are held by the Thatcham Angling Association. The ponds were cleaned and re-stocked in 1977. They contain chub, perch, roach, bream, tench and carp.

The upper fish pond

14. Wellingtonia. *Sequoiadendron gigantium.* These were introduced to Britain in 1858 from the west coast of North America. Although the longest lived species is the Bristlecone Pine, the Wellingtonia species includes some of the largest and oldest trees in the world. The largest Wellingtonia is thought to be 'General Sherman' which is growing on the west coast of the USA and is over 350

The dam

feet (107m) tall and 3,500 years old. Even if planted soon after introduction, the six trees on the Common can be barely 150 years old and yet they already dominate the skyline. Note the many nest holes in their soft bark.

15. Bilberries. These are another plant of acid heathlands. The small blue berries were, and are, picked to make pies and sauces but it takes a very long time to gather enough!

16. Pillow Mounds. These, too, were built by Reading Abbey, probably in the 13th century. Rabbits are not native to Britain, they were introduced from Sicily by the Normans and the first reference to them is on the Isles of Scilly. There was a coney garth at Guildford in 1235. They were initially unable to cope with the British climate. Artificial warrens were created for them from which they were netted using ferrets. The mounds are called pillow mounds. The netting seems to have been one of the duties of the ladies. The rabbit was a very valuable animal; the fur was used to line winter clothing and the

| *Bilberry* | *Cross leaved heath* | *Lichen cladonia portentosa* |

flesh was considered a delicacy. Warreners' houses were often strongly built to resist attack by gangs seeking to steal the pelts.

17. World War 2 remains. This road was part of the storage area used to stockpile military stores ahead of the D-Day invasion. Buried in the undergrowth to the north are the footings of an extensive encampment which housed the people servicing the stores. After the war the huts were taken over by people who had been bombed out of their homes and by demobilised soldiers for whom there were no houses. The huts were in poor condition and the squatters suffered severely from cold and a fire killed a baby. They were eventually re-housed and the huts demolished.

Sources and further reading

Victoria County History – Berkshire

Morris J (Ed)	*Domesday Book – Berkshire* Phillimore 1979
Ekwall E (Ed)	*The Concise Dictionary of English Place-names* OUP 1974
Mabey R	*Flora Britannica* Chatto & Windus 1997
Williamson T	*Shaping Medieval Landscapes* Windgather Press 2003
Rackham O	*The History of the Countryside* Dent 1986
Rackham O	*Woodlands* Harper Collins 2006
Millson C	*Bucklebury's Heritage* Privately published 1994
Humphries AL	*Bucklebury* Privately published 1932
Rocque J	*A Survey of the County of Berkshire* 1761 reprinted c.1975

CHAPTER TWELVE

Water meadows, lost roads & green lanes
Exploring the fields and woods between Stanford Dingley and Frilsham Common

Water meadows. Water meadows were introduced in the late 15th century and are not just wet fields near streams! They are carefully engineered with dams and with complex sets of flooding and draining ditches. These allowed a thin film of river water to be passed over the grass in the early spring. The water flowing out of the chalk through springs into the river would be warmer than the surface and would contain chalk sediment. The water warmed and fertilised the ground producing an early growth of grass on which ewes were fed before lambing. The sheep trod their dung into the land thus increasing its fertility. When the grass in other pastures became available the ewes and their lambs were moved out and the meadow closed to grow hay.

Rents for these fields were very high. Management of water meadows was very skilled and labour intensive. The operators were known as 'drowners.'

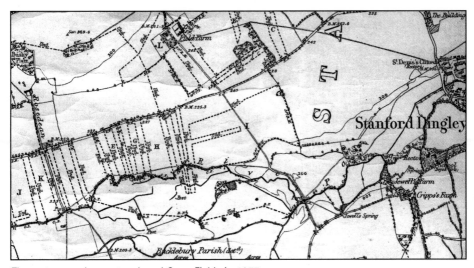

The water meadow network and Open Fields in 1877

The meadows ceased to be maintained during the agricultural depression at the end of the 19th century. There are many sites along the lower Pang Valley. The area between Stanford Dingley and Bucklebury is particularly rich in remains of the dams and sluices.

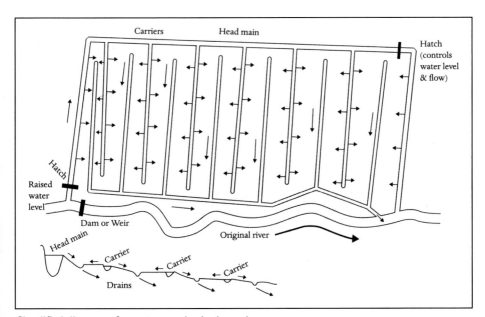

Simplified diagram of a water meadow's channels

Medieval roads. Roads are some of the oldest features in the landscape. Many were certainly in existence over a thousand years ago because they are recorded as boundary features in Saxon Charters. Many are much older than this and may have originated as trackways in the Neolithic and Bronze Ages and thus be as much as five or six thousand years old. These are the ones which follow natural routes such as along ridges or up valley bottoms.

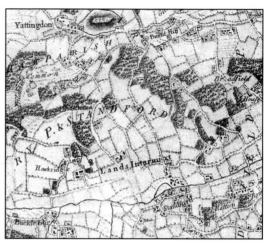

Rocque's Survey of Berkshire 1761

Road maintenance was the responsibility of individual parishes until the County Councils took over main roads in 1889 and Rural Districts took over minor roads in 1894. Parishes did the minimum possible in order to keep down the Parish Rate and all roads were atrocious. William Cobbett (1830) reports that when using roads in clay areas the liquid mud was often up to his horse's belly and that some horses could not be made to use the road. This made road transport slow and expensive.

In the late 1700's Turnpike Trusts started to construct the first built roads in this country since the Roman Period. (See chapter 14). These were toll roads and expensive to use. Most people continued to use the old roads. The Industrial Revolution put more pressure on the road network and the

Length men c 1930

demand for better roads grew during the 19th century. Councils either built new roads or improved the drainage and surfaces of old ones. They employed 'length men' who were allocated a section of road to maintain. John Rocque's *Survey of Berkshire* in 1761 shows the medieval roads just before the period of improvement.

Enclosures. Medieval farming using Open Fields divided into acre and half acre strips was very inefficient. From as early as the 13th century Open Fields were enclosed with hedges and allocated to individual farmers following local agreements. In the late 18th century Acts of Parliament were passed to speed up this process and most Open Fields had disappeared by the late 19th century. (See Chapter 4).

From fields to woodland. The hedges lining the new Turnpikes and the newly enclosed fields had to be protected with hazel hurdles until they were established. Many less fertile fields were planted up as hazel coppices to provide the hurdles. These new coppices can be detected by their poor ground flora. Old coppices are rich in Ancient Woodland Indicator Species such as bluebell, wood anemone and early purple orchids.

An ancient swallow hole now blocked with clay revealed in a quarry

Swallow Holes. These are breaks in the surface strata which allow water to penetrate into the underlying permeable rock rather than run along the surface as streams and rivers.

There are many swallow holes in this part of the downland dip slope and three can be seen from this walk. The whole area is a complex of thin horizontal layers of clays and gravels known as the Reading Formation. At the swallow hole sites a layer of impervious clay overlies gravels which in turn overlie chalk. Rain falling on the clay runs off down small channels onto the gravel where it sinks into the ground to join an aquifer. The chalk underlying the dip slope is heavily fissured with gaps and joints. Over time the water running through a regular set of joints dissolves the chalk and widens the passageway. The water drains down to the groundwater table which is the upper limit of the saturated chalk known as an aquifer. If the passage becomes big enough the surface may collapse into it and form a cone shaped pit. These pits have often been quarried as a source of road making material and have thus been enlarged. A swallow hole can easily be confused with a quarry.

The best example of the process in the Pang Valley is provided by the Blue Pools (See Chapter 13) between Stanford Dingley and Bradfield. In the 1980s the owner realised that the Pools became turbid about sixteen hours after a period of heavy rain. Hydro-geologists who investigated the problem found that silt and other pollutants collected by rain water flowing into swallow holes at Holly Lane and Tylers Lane, Bucklebury, five and a half kilometres to the west of the Pools was the source of the turbidity. This was proved by adding harmless fluorescein dye to the water collecting in the holes which was duly observed in the Pools sixteen and a half hours later.

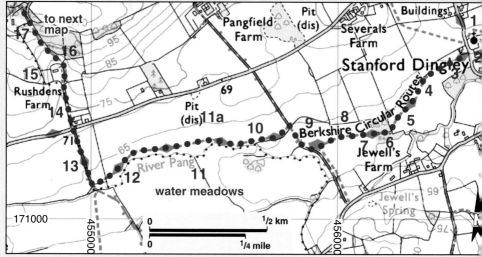

This walk runs from Stanford Dingley to the Pot Kiln on Frilsham Common and back, through water meadows, green lanes and woods. It starts and finishes at Stanford Dingley church. There is an optional shorter route.

- The full walk is about 5 miles or 8 km long and the shorter walk is about 3½ miles or 6km long. Both routes are along wide, clear and well-marked tracks.
- There are several stiles and a short steep hill and surfaces can be uneven and muddy.
- There are two road crossings and two short lengths of road walking.
- Horses and riders may be encountered.
- Beware of electric fences in the grazing paddocks. Only cross at the insulated spaces

Ordnance Survey maps Explorer 159 'Reading' or Explorer 158 'Newbury and Hungerford' will be useful.

Stanford Dingley. The place name means *stoney ford* and is listed in Domesday Book. *Dingley* comes from Robert Dyngley who held the manor in 1428. There was certainly a settlement here much earlier. The name is Saxon and Roman remains have been found locally.

1. Stanford Dingley church. Is dedicated to St Denys who was also the patron saint of France. The church is reputed to have been built in Saxon times and to incorporate some of the old church. The font is Norman and the door dates from the 13th century. There are 13th century wall paintings. Like most ancient churches it has been extended and repaired many times.

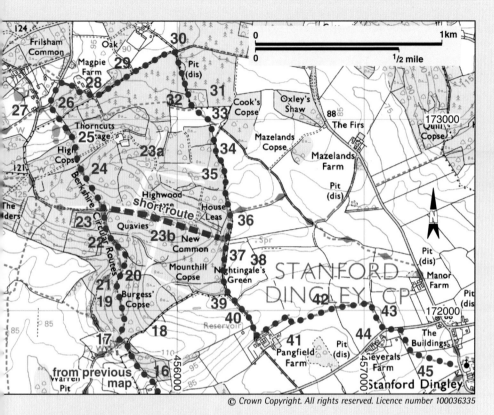

2. Stanford Dingley Manor. The original manor house was surrounded by a moat which can still be traced in part. The 15th century Yattendon manor house is similar.

3. Fish ponds. The hollows near the road are reputed to be fish ponds.

4. Old stream channels. These channels were probably fed from springs in the hill side. The general lowering of the water table due to modern water extraction has stopped them flowing.

5. Industrial site. These rectangular pits are not mentioned in any document so far found. They are too small for fish ponds and may be flax or hemp retting ponds. Both flax and hemp plants were rotted in water to release the fibres for making linen, rope and coarse cloth. The channels extend into the alder coppice and must therefore be older than the coppice, which itself contains a wide range of Ancient Woodland Indicator Species.

6. Alder coppice. Alder was a valuable tree. It grew in land that was too wet to cultivate and produced poles for scaffolding, gunpowder, dyes, clog soles and underwater piling. The coppice has many Ancient Woodland Indicators.

Look for: bluebell, Solomon's seal, wood sorrel, enchanter's nightshade, yellow archangel and flag iris.

7. Wet meadow. This is valuable for wetland plants. Look for, in season: common and marsh mallow, yarrow, silverweed and buttercups.

8. Wetland. Look for sallow, alder and willow, sedges and flag iris.

9 & 10. Water Lane & ponds. The lane is an ancient north south route. The ponds are modern.

11. Water meadow. The note on the main page describes these. The 1877 map shows them in their decline. The twisting channels to the south of the river are the remains of the flooding and draining channels. The channel on the south side of the field collected the water and returned it to the river lower down stream.

The northern channel was dredged and re-graded in the 1980's to improve land drainage. Look for black medic, teasels, comfrey, bladder campion. The exotic shrubs were planted to mitigate the effects of the dredging. Look for spindle, waxberry and dogwood.

11a. Open Field. The field to the north was an open field farmed in strips and shared by both Stanford Dingley and Bucklebury. Such sharing frequently indicates that both were once a single estate.

Solomon's seal & bluebells

12. Sluice & dam site. The dam raised the water level sufficiently to flood the fields through sluices in the bank. Look further west along the river bank for some rare black poplars.

13. Ancient trackway. The southern part of this track is not shown in 1761 but the northern part is. The ages are confirmed by the hedges. The south is species poor but the drive edge contains ancient oak trees

Water meadow sluice at Point 12

Guidance note: The Right of Way runs up the drive, not along the field edge.

14. Ancient pollard oak. Its 4.05m girth indicates an age of about 300 years

Guidance note: The Right of Way has been officially diverted. It now runs to the east of the farm.

15. Rushdens Farm. (Rosedean in 1877). The name means rushy hollow. It is probably an ancient spring line settlement and is shown on the 1761 map. The west end of the house looks older than the rest. The new path route actually follows the 1763 route which led to open grazing land further north.

16. Hazel coppice & old road. This coppice is shown in 1761 and is probably as ancient as the settlement. Farmers in the era before the introduction of barbed wire, plastic and electric fences required large quantities of sticks, poles and larger timber to make hurdles for fences, tools and buildings and for firewood. This was provided by coppices. They were usually hazel and ash but other trees were used. The coppices were inter-planted with standard trees, usually oak or ash to supply larger timber. Coppicing involves cutting off the tree near ground level and allowing it to produce multiple shoots which are then harvested at short intervals. This cutting and lack of soil disturbance produces the rich flora.

17. Ancient field maple stool.

Guidance note: Go left across the bank and turn right along the path

18. Ancient bank & ditch. This is the parish boundary and is likely to be at least 1100 years old. Parish boundaries were generally fixed in the 9th century. The parish priest guarded them since the area they enclosed determined his income from the Tithe. They were often the boundaries of earlier estates and some have been shown to go back to the Bronze Age and thus be over 4000 years old. (See Chapter 5).

19. Saw pit. Before the days of diesel tractors, trees were often cut up in the woods to make them easier to move. This pit would have been about 6 feet deep with boarded sides. The saw was worked by one man standing on the log and another in the pit. They cut the tree lengthways into planks and beams.

20. Rhododendron. These were introduced in the 19th century as ornamental plants and as cover for pheasants. They were actually native before the last Ice Age. They belong to the heather family and spread rapidly by seed and sucker on acid soils wiping out all existing ground flora.

21. Gravel pit. This was probably for road building material.

22. Double planted beech. Sometimes these double trees result from two seeds in a squirrel's hoard.

23. Pond. This probably pre-dates the woods and was made to water stock in the old fields shown in 1761.

Parting of the Ways. Turn right for the shorter route.

23a. Pond. This pond is fed from the gravels and drains into the swallow hole at 35.

23b. New Common. This may have been allocated when the fields were enclosed as part of a negotiated enclosure settlement.

Ash stool near Point 28 7m girth over 700 years old

24. Fields converted to coppice. This area was covered with fields in 1761. The new woods are species poor except along the old hedges.

25. Saw pit & potash pit. Twigs, bracken and waste wood were burned to make potash. Lye, made by soaking the wood ash, was boiled with animal fats and lime to make soap. The residue was used in the glass making process. Imported North American potash destroyed the market for domestic potash in about 1830 and its manufacture in English woods largely stopped. Therefore potash pits indicate old copses.

Old ash stool near Point 34 4.17m girth probably over 400 years old

26. Species rich hedge. Look for hawthorn, blackthorn, crab, field maple, cherry, ash, hazel, elder, holly. It is also a valuable linking route.

27. The Pot Kiln pub. This was built to serve thirsty brick makers. The brick kiln was at the rear of the pub.

28. Magpie Farm. Originally *Franklin's Farm*. A franklin was a free man who owned his farm rather than holding from the lord of the manor. Two free men are recorded for the Manor of Frilsham in Domesday Book. It is a very ancient settlement.

29. Swallow holes & species rich verge. These holes are formed by rain water

Swallow hole near Point 35

running off the clay on to gravel covered chalk. The chalk dissolves and the surface collapses to form a pit. On the verge look for mallow, agrimony, yarrow, scabious, campion, tansy, bedstraw & others.

30. Old road. This is the original Yattendon to Stanford Dingley road. It is also the parish boundary and so at least 1000 years old.

31. Pond. Probably artificial.

32. Swallow hole.

33. Old roads. These are shown in 1761 as important roads.

34. Ancient stools. The banks are lined with ash stools resulting from centuries of cutting.

35. Deep swallow hole. This fed from the pond at 23a

36. House Leas. The 1761 map shows a widened road and houses. In 1877 there was a settlement called *Dodd's Cottages.*

37. Old road. Note that the road banks are now closer together.

38. Nightingales Green. The widened track was the 'green' for this old settlement. It had disappeared before Rocque did his survey in 1761.

39. Parish boundary bank & ditch. This is another part of the bank we saw at 17. The ditch marks the boundary.

40. Old road. Note how deeply it is cut into the landscape.

41. Pangfield Farm. Originally *Field Farm* it was probably built when the Open Fields were enclosed. This was before 1761.

42. Open Fields. The species poor hedges indicate that they are relatively young and were planted when the fields were enclosed

43. Double boundary. This is the southern end of the road to Yattendon. Note the hollow way running to the north from the path corner.

44. Severall's Farm. The name indicates a farm that was held as a unit, not in strips. The buildings are not shown in 1877.

45. Electric fences. This is a dairy farm so beware the electric fences. Only cross at the protected places.

Sources and further reading

Victoria County History – Berkshire

Morris J (Ed)	*Domesday Book – Berkshire*	Phillimore 1979
Wood M	*Domesday – a search for the roots of England*	BBC 1986
Ekwall E (Ed)	*The Concise Dictionary of English Place-names*	OUP 1974
Mabey R	*Flora Britannica*	Chatto & Windus 1997
Williamson T	*Shaping Medieval Landscapes*	Windgather Press 2003
Greenaway D & Ward D	*In the Valley of the Pang*	The Friends of the Pang and Kennet Valleys 2002
Rackham O	*The History of the Countryside*	Dent 1986
Rackham O	*Woodlands*	Harper Collins 2006
Rocque J	*A Survey of the County of Berkshire*	1761 reprinted c.1975
Everard M (et al)	*Water meadows*	Forrest Text 2005
Cobbett W	*Rural Rides*	Everyman' Library Dent 1957

CHAPTER THIRTEEN

Down the Pang
Exploring the northern part of Bradfield parish

New bridge
above Blue Pool 11.7.03

The Blue Pools. The Pools are the perennial head of the River Pang. During the 1980's and again in the first years of this century and at other recorded periods in history, the channel dried-up upstream of Stanford Dingley, but in the driest years the river still flows from the Blue Pools.

The Pools are fed by artesian springs as shown in the diagram. Rain falling on the chalk hills along the valley sides forms a water table higher than the chalk surface in the valley bottom. The impervious Reading Formations cover the lower valley sides and so a head of water exists which forces water to the surface in the valley bottom. The artesian pressure results in the shimmering jets of sand and water visible in the pools. Other springs exist in the bed of the river but are not so obvious.

The Blue Pool springs contribute over 50% of the river flow and produce a steady 0.2 cubic metres of water per second at 10 degrees Celsius winter and summer. The lowest recorded flow was 0.086 cubic metres per second in July 1976 during one of the severest drought periods on record.

In its passage through the clay the water collects clay particles and these cause light to be defracted at the blue end of the spectrum thus producing the vivid blue colours seen on a sunny day. Algal growth adds a greenish tint.

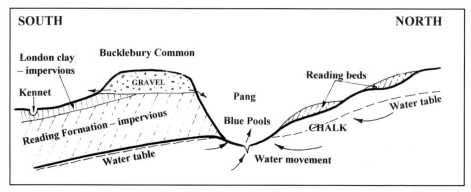

Schemmatic section through the Blue Pools

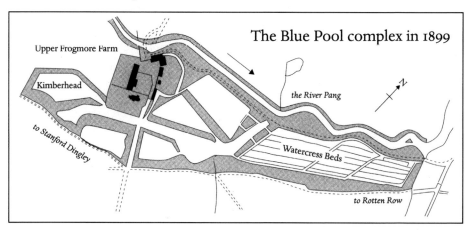

A small spring has existed here since before the first maps were made, but the site was only developed in the mid to late 19th century when the pools were dug to grow watercress. To improve the flow, five or six narrow diameter boreholes were driven through the clay layer and sparkling water from these can be seen irrupting through the beds of the pools.

In the 1980's, as more fully described in the previous chapter, it was recognised that the pools became turbid about 16 hours after rainfall. This was traced to pollution from two natural swallow holes at Holly Lane and Tylers Lane. In 1987 the local Environmental Health Department found faecal contamination during routine testing and decided that the water was too polluted for watercress growing to continue and the cress beds were abandoned. The current owners have tried very hard to trace and cure the pollution but have not succeeded, and the site is now managed for the benefit of wildlife.

Watermills. The Pang's power has been used to drive mills from very early times. Domesday Book records mills at Yattendon, Frilsham, Bucklebury, Stanford [Dingley], Bradfield and Pangbourne. At a later date there was even a mill of some sort at Compton driven by the tiny northern branch of the Pang. In 1329 a mill was built at Tidmarsh for Reading Abbey. The mill buildings at Frilsham, Stanford Dingley, Bradfield and Tidmarsh still exist, although converted to other uses, and at Bucklebury a water wheel can still be seen which was used to drive fans and machinery in the iron foundry.

There are several different types of watermill and the type chosen depends on the topography. Water rushing down a steep channel can be used to drive a wheel laid horizontally by directing a jet on to one side of the wheel. Very early mills seem to be of this type because the vertical axle could drive the stones directly without the need for bevelled gearing.

The main requirement at a mill site is a good 'head of water'. The head of water is the difference in height between the water upstream of the mill and at the tail of the mill. The greater the head the greater the potential energy available. A head can be achieved by taking water out of a river channel upstream of the mill and then leading it along a channel following the valley side contours. This channel is called a leat and the leat supplying Bradfield mill is visible from this walk. The water in the original channel continues to fall as it flows down hill until at the mill site there is a considerable difference in level between the two channels. Water from the leat can then be directed on to a vertical waterwheel where it either fills up troughs fitted around the circumference or pushes against paddles. The greater the radius of the wheel the greater the turning force on the axle. This, too, is a function of the difference in water levels. Very small trickles of water can supply surprising amounts of power if they can be led from far enough up the valley to provide a large head and thus allow a wheel with a large radius.

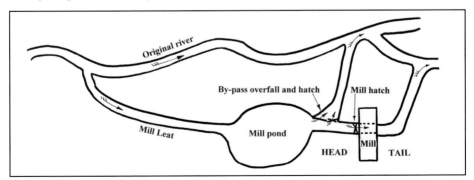

Diagram of a watermill system

At the mill site water from the leat may be collected in a mill pool to act as a reserve supply to extend the milling time. The water is controlled by a system of sluices and overfalls to allow the mill to be stopped and to be isolated for repairs.

Once the channels were constructed mills were rebuilt repeatedly on the same site. Deserted sites can often be identified from the surviving channel pattern.

Ownership of a mill was a valuable resource for the Lord of a Manor as he could require suit of mill of his tenants forcing them to grind their corn at his mill and to pay for the privilege. Millers throughout folklore have a bad name for greed and extortion!

A decline in local milling took place after the repeal of the Corn Laws in 1846. These laws had protected British wheat from competition but had resulted in very high bread prices. After this, harder, drier grain was imported from North America and milled in large factory mills at the dock side. Water millers tried to diversify to survive. Some mills drove electricity generators and an attempt was made at Bradfield to power a refrigeration plant. At Tidmarsh Mill new equipment was fitted but the windows fell out when it was started up!

This walk includes the River Pang and Bradfield. It starts and finishes at Rushall Manor Farm.

- **It is about 5 miles or 8 km long. The route is along wide, clear and well marked tracks.**
- **There are two modest hills and several stiles. Surfaces can be uneven and muddy.**
- **There are three road crossings and one short length of road walking.**
- **Horses and riders may be encountered.**

Ordnance Survey map Explorer 159 'Reading' will be useful.

1. Rushall Manor Farm. The 18th century Black Barn and other old farm buildings have been restored and converted for use as a centre for the John Simonds Educational Trust. The farm is used to introduce children and young people to the countryside and receives many school visits and youth camping parties every year. The Trust has a strong religious focus.

2. Species rich hedges. Please note that the footpath has been officially diverted. The first hedge has at least 10 species indicating great age. The second, which was a parish boundary, has at least 8 species. However, in

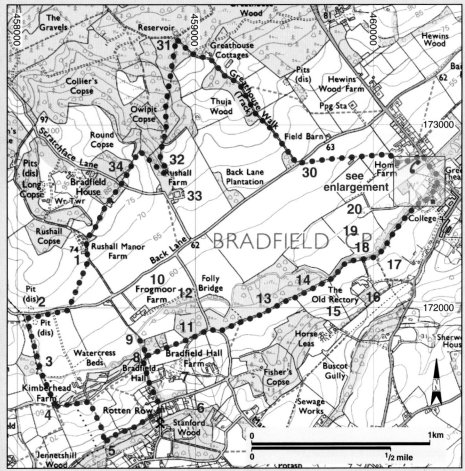

spring, bluebells in the hedge bottoms show that both hedges are relics of ancient woodland and not planted hedges. Look for blackthorn, hawthorn, elm, field maple, hazel, briar, dogwood, spindle, oak and ash.

3. River Pang. Note the wet meadows on either side and the raised bank on the south side. Look in the river for water mint, water forget-me-not, water crowfoot, water cress, water dropwort... and on the banks for willow herb, comfrey, silverweed, meadowsweet, hemlock, hedge cranesbill, tufted vetch, great burnet, black medick, marsh bedstraw, yellow vetchling...

4. Kimberhead. The place name means *Cyneburg's Spring* and *Cyneburg* is a Saxon woman's name. It was also known as *The Rising* and *The Blue Pool*. The western end, where a view point has been provided, is the original pool. The

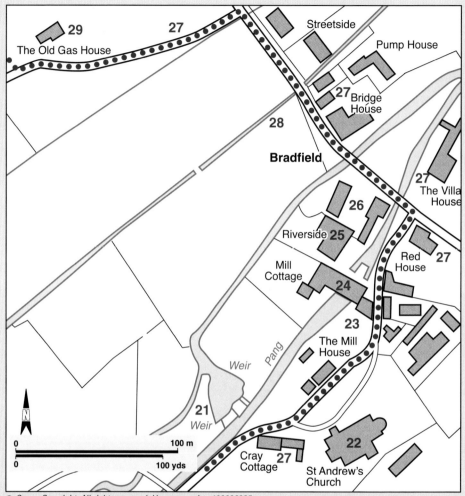

main notes provide more information. The other ponds were developed for watercress and the cottage was built as a summer refuge from Bradfield Hall in the late 19th century.

5. Jennetshill Wood. This track is an ancient road shown on the earliest maps. It provides an excellent view over the valley. Look for horsetail, wood sorrel, herb Robert.. The flora indicates an ancient wood. Look for: wood mellick, wood sedge, wood spurge ...

6. Rotten Row. The name may mean *Riders Row* and seems to apply to the string of ancient settlement along the edge of Bradfield Hall Park. This string is probably a medieval green settlement on the edge of the former Bradfield

Water crowsfoot　　　　　*Hemlock water dropwort*　　　　*Flag iris*

Common which was situated around Bradfield Southend. A Primitive Methodist chapel existed here before 1830 and in 1851 attracted 96 people to its evening meeting. 'Slipper Cottage' and 'Farthings' were both pubs and 'Farthings' housed a shoemaker who employed three men. Note the Victorian letterbox – still in use.

7. Bradfield Hall. Originally built in 1763 by John Barrington (said to be an illegitimate son of George II) for his eldest son (also illegitimate) on condition that he, too, never married.

8. Confluence of spring and river.

9. Dipping Platform, alders & ford. The platform was provided to allow school parties to investigate the ecology of the river. Note the large alder coppice stools. Alder was a very valuable wood, it made the high grade charcoal used to make gunpowder; it provided light long straight scaffold poles and rot resistant underwater piling and it also provided a red dye from its sap and a green dye from its leaves. Finally, in the words of Kipling *'alder for shoes do wise men use...'* it made good clog soles.

The solar panels at the ford power a river monitor which transmits direct to the Environment Agency.

10. (Lower) Frogmore Farm. Dates from at least the 17th century. In the 1890's the tenant managed the watercress beds. The original bridge was in front of the house and was part of an ancient north–south route. In the 1970's there was a successful vineyard which relied on boys from Bradfield College to pick the grapes.

Guidance Note: Return to the main path at Point 8.

11. Wet meadows. Now planted with poplars and managed by grazing.

12. Folly Bridge. Rebuilt in 1947 after floods swept away the original hump-backed bridge.

13. Long Meadow Plantation. This is a valuable wetland habitat. It has many drainage ditches and the flora indicates that part of it is Ancient Secondary Woodland. It is a hazel and alder coppice with oak standards. A few Scots pines have also been planted. The coppicing was sold in 1948 for £5. There is also some valuable standing deadwood. Deadwood provides a home for the fungi, bacteria and mini-beasts which are at the bottom of the food chain and without which there would be no larger birds and mammals. **Without dead wood your wood would be dead!** Note the sharp drop from the field into the coppice caused by a build up of plough soil. Look for yellow flag iris....

Coppiced alder

14. Veteran oaks. The eastern of these two magnificent trees measures 4.39m in girth and is thus about 270 years old; the western is about the same age. They are growing in an ideal site on the edge of acid clay with plenty of water available.

15. The College golf course. This has fairly recently been created on the Old Rectory Meadows and ensures that they remain as

Oak at Point 14

grassland. Hopefully areas of 'rough' will be allowed to harbour some of the surviving old grassland plants. The trees on the skyline are the remains of a lime avenue planted in 1866. The younger trees nearer the wood were planted in the mid 20th century to maintain a parkland appearance.

16. The Old Rectory. This was built in the 1880's to replace an even older rectory which had been home for over 100 years to successive Stevens family rectors. The last, Thomas Stevens, was rector from 1842 to 1881. He founded Bradfield College in 1850. In 1881 he was bankrupted and he and his family were evicted.

Kingcups   Brooklime

17. College playing fields. These have grown with the College size.

18. Mill leat. This is an artificial channel dug at a very early date as part of the watermill complex. It carries water along the contour to the mill and thus creates a head of water to drive the wheel.

19. Water meadows. These fields are visibly lower than the leat. They were carefully flooded each spring to warm and fertilise the soil so as to provide an early crop of grass for lambing ewes. They had fallen into disuse by the early 20th century and were ploughed up during World War 2. Water meadows were carefully engineered with flooding channels, drains and sluices which allowed a controlled film of water to run over the ground. They produced rich crops of hay and rents were high, but they were labour intensive and went out of use during the late 19th century agricultural depression.

20. Outers. This is the site of the College out-door swimming pool. It was fed by the original river channel which also drained the water-meadows.

21. Mill by-pass sluices. The overfall and sluice allowed water to by-pass the mill when it was not required to drive the wheel.

22. St Andrew's Church. The brick and flint tower is 16th century, but the rest was mostly rebuilt in the 1840's by Thomas Stevens. It was designed by Gilbert Scott.

23. Mill House. Built in the 18th century. It has a lean-to which once housed the village shop and post office.

24. Bradfield Mill. A mill is recorded in Domesday Book but the present building is Victorian. It was built when the watermill was enlarged and converted from being a corn mill to being a pumping station supplying water from St Andrew's Well to the College, village and workhouse. In the 1870's an attempt was made to install a turbine to power refrigeration plant but the attempt failed.

25. Village school. This is dated 1862 and is now the College art studio.

26. Mill Cottages. These old houses were acquired by the local authority in the 1950's and converted to house retired and elderly people.

27. Georgian houses. These all pre-date the dominant brick & flint of the College, but would have been in keeping with the Old Rectory.

Bradfield Mill

28. Original course of the river.

29. The Gas House. Designed by Gilbert Scott and built in 1867 to house plant producing gas to light the College, the church and the rectory. It stopped production when the rector became bankrupt in 1881

Bradfield mill sluices

and for a term the College had to use 500 oil lamps. Electricity was installed 40 years later and the building was converted to a house. The Gilbert Scott façade was retained.

30. Fields. Presumably these were the 'Broad Fields' from which the village gets its name. Most of the fields from Bradfield to Stanford Dingley are managed organically.

31. Great House Woods. These are flower rich Ancient Secondary Woodland. The woods are mostly hazel coppice with oak standards. In Spring look for violets, celandines, bluebells, yellow archangel, yellow pimpernel, wood spurge, wood anemone.......

32. Owl Pit Quarry. This was started in 1830 to provide chalk to sweeten the acid soils of the surrounding fields. It is a Regionally Important Geological Site (RIGS) and an excellent interpretation board has been provided to explain the features in the exposed chalk face.

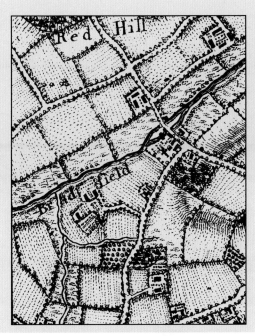

Bradfield in 1761

33. Rushall Farm. Built after the original Manor Farm burned down.
34. Coppices. These hazel coppices are Ancient Woodland and have a very rich flora. In Spring: look for:- bluebells, Solomon's seal, yellow archangel, wood anemone...

Sources and further reading

Victoria County History – Berkshire

Morris J (Ed)	*Domesday Book – Berkshire*	Phillimore 1979
Wood M	*Domesday – a search for the roots of England*	BBC 1986
Ekwall E (Ed)	*The Concise Dictionary of English Place-names*	OUP 1974
Ward D (Analysis)	*Census Returns 1851*	Personal communication
Ward D (Analysis)	*Tithe Commutation Award & Map*	Personal communication
Mabey R	*Flora Britannica*	Chatto & Windus 1997
Williamson T	*Shaping Medieval Landscapes*	Windgather Press 2003
Greenaway D & Ward D	*In the Valley of the Pang*	The Friends of the Pang and Kennet Valleys 2002
Rackham O	*The History of the Countryside*	Dent 1986
Rackham O	*Woodlands*	Harper Collins 2006
Rocque J	*A Survey of the County of Berkshire 1761*	reprinted c.1975
Wailes R	*A Source Book of Windmills and Watermills*	Ward Lock Ltd 1979

CHAPTER FOURTEEN

Turnpikes & tank traps
Exploring the lower Pang Valley

The Sulham Gap. The Pang Valley between the M4 and the Thames is known as the Sulham Gap.

As the last Ice Age was ending about 10,000 years ago, the River Kennet, which ran through the Gap to join the Thames near the site of the future Pangbourne, suddenly switched its main course and ran through the Coley Gap to join the Thames at its modern confluence. The reason for the switch is not known, but the modern watershed between the two rivers, now followed by the old A4, is very low and a blockage of the Kennet could easily return it to its old course. The Pang, which had originally joined the Kennet at Tidmarsh, continued to flow down the old channel, but could only provide a small fraction of the previous volume of water. The greater volume of water provided by the Kennet had cut out a wide flood plain which has hardly changed since it was abandoned. Earlier down-cutting by the Kennet had created gravel terraces on either side of the valley. The continuous wide terrace along the north side of the Kennet valley and the east side of the gap, along which the Theale to Tidmarsh turnpike runs, provides strong evidence for the change of direction. The Moors are in the floodplain and the villages are on the terraces.

Medieval Land Reclamation. The drainage of wetlands has a long history in this country. The Romans were experts and had carried out major schemes all over their empire. The emperor Hadrian, as well as building The Wall to mark the frontier of Roman Britain, also built the great drainage channel known as the Car Dyke in East Anglia. This is nearly 90 miles (144km) long and runs along the western edge of the fens.

Land reclamation is expensive and only major landowners had the necessary capital. The most enthusiastic drainers were the religious orders who had the funds and the continuity of management required to carry through major schemes. Although there is no documentary evidence, it is reasonable to suspect that Reading Abbey drained the marshes around Tidmarsh soon after they acquired the manor in the 12th century. The grid of wide ditches and the raising of the river bank is likely to be their work. Nevertheless, the Moors were still known as 'The common marsh of Pangborne' in 1634 and are shown as 'a Common' in 1761.

Wet meadows were very valuable because they provided the hay needed to keep livestock, particularly the plough oxen, alive during the winter and rents were therefore much higher.

They are also botanically interesting because the 'islands' created by the new channels are acid while the channels themselves are alkaline. One 'island' has been designated as a Site of Special Scientific Interest (SSSI) as unimproved lowland acid grassland and for its population of harebells, dwarf gorse and petty whin.

Turnpike Roads. (See also Chapter 12) Medieval roads were atrocious. Some Roman Roads still survived and were used but most roads were muddy tracks. William Cobbett writing in the 1830's often describes riding along roads with mud up to his horse's belly.

The area in 1761

A law passed in 1555 put the responsibility for road maintenance on parishes. They were required to elect a Surveyor of the Highways and every male in the parish was required to provide four consecutive days labour (later six days) without pay to repair the roads. This Statute Labour was bitterly resented, the work was done half-heartedly and avoided whenever possible.

Turnpike road at Englefield

The 18th century demand for improved transport resulted in the creation of Turnpike Trusts which undertook to build and maintain certain roads in return for the tolls. There was furious resistance from many different lobbies, even to the extent of attacking and burning the gates. Part of the Great North Road was the first to be turnpiked in 1663 and the Bath Road followed in 1706. A turnpike road from Pangbourne to the Bath Road was built in the late 1700s with a toll house at Tidmarsh.

Turnpike milestone.

The most obvious signs of a turnpike road are long straight stretches of road with identical milestones and occasional toll houses. Toll houses usually stand immediately at the roadside and are often decoratively built.

County Councils took over the construction and maintenance of main roads in 1889 and of local roads in 1894. Stand in the Moor Copse car park and you can see three generations of road history. The original medieval road from Theale via North Street, now a green lane, the late 18th century turnpike to the Bath Road and the M4 motorway.

Type 28A pillbox

Two pounder anti-tank gun
Image courtesy of the Royal Artillary Historical Trust

Stop Line GHQ Red. In 1940, during World War 2 and after the retreat from Dunkirk, the German army was expected to invade southern England. They had demonstrated the use of fast moving groups of tanks to break up defending forces in Poland and later during the Blitzkrieg which led to the fall of Holland, Belgium and France. They were expected to use the same technique in Britain.

To counter this threat a number of 'Stop Lines' were constructed to hold up the tanks. Stop Line GHQ Red ran from the Kennet at Theale Mill to the Thames close to the east of Pangbourne. It consisted of a deep ditch covered by a large number of concrete gun positions. These were known as Type 28A pillboxes and were constructed by local building contractors. Messrs Smallbone of Streatley built many of the Pangbourne pill boxes. Each pillbox housed a 2 pound anti-tank gun and light machine guns.

The ditch ended ten yards short of the River Thames and rapidly filled with water. A local boy once caught a sizeable pike in it! The ditch was backfilled soon after the end of the war but the gun positions still exist. At least one of them has been converted to a garden shed. *Swords into plough shares!*

The defences would probably have been rather ineffective because the enemy had captured many of the two pounder guns in the early stages of the war and had designed their armour accordingly. A six pounder gun was under development but it was decided that there was not time to re-tool the factories to make it and the two pounder gun had to be retained. Fortunately neither gun was needed!

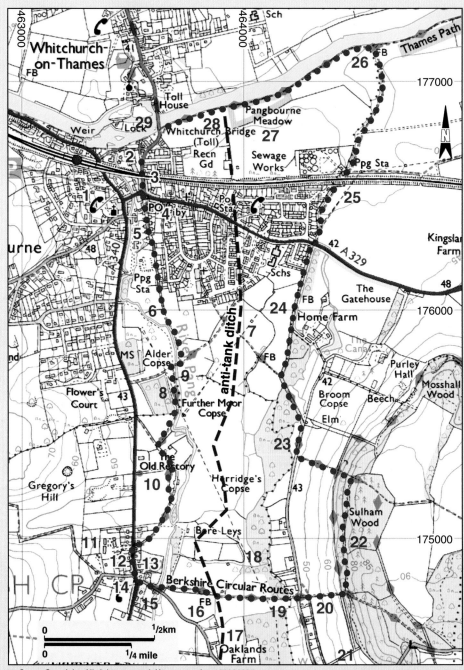

This walk includes Pangbourne, Tidmarsh and Sulham. It runs via The Moors, Tidmarsh village and Sulham Woods. It starts and finishes at Pangbourne.

- It is about 3½ miles or 6 km long. The route is along wide, clear and well marked tracks.
- There are several stiles and a modest hill and surfaces can be uneven and muddy.
- There are four road crossings and two lengths of road walking. The pavements in Tidmarsh village are very narrow and the road is busy.
- Horses and riders may be encountered.

Ordnance Survey map Explorer 159 'Reading' will be useful.

1. Pangbourne Village. There was a Roman settlement at Pangbourne and Domesday Book records two manors and two mills. One of these may have been near the Pang's confluence with the Thames.

2. Working Men's Club. Founded in the 1890's with premises near the station, the Club bought 'Roselea' in 1900. The house dates from the early 19th century. The Club almost lost the premises when their mortgage was called in but were saved by a Pangbourne businessman (Mr A Petrocokino) who paid off the mortgage and presented the house to the club.

3. The Railway. Isambard Brunel built the Great Western Railway. It opened to Reading on 30 March 1840 and had passed Pangbourne by July 1840. It was initially Broad Gauge. Note the two phases of building in the bridge.

4. The School. Now 'Premier' and 'Garlands'. The 'Breedon School' was established in 1684 as a charity by the will of John Breedon of Bere Court and was to be a school for 12 boys – 'particularly those of the poorer sort.' It continued until 1900 when a school was built on Pangbourne Hill. In 1890 there was fierce opposition to the vicar and the school master who were refusing to accept boys who had not been baptised.

5. Pangbourne Mill (site). Probably on the same site as one of the Domesday mills, it had two waterwheels and four

Pangbourne Mill

pairs of millstones. From 1871 it was tenanted by the Stone family who later bought it. A water pumping station was built on part of the site in 1929. A mill was a very valuable asset to a Lord of a Manor since his tenants were required to use it and to pay for the privilege. They were not allowed to grind their corn at home or outside the manor.

6. Perched river banks. The river banks have been deliberately raised to allow the water level upstream of the mill to be maintained at a higher level than normal. This provided more power to the mill and allowed it to grind for longer.

7. The Sulham Gap. The Pang Valley between the M4 and the Thames is known as the Sulham Gap.

As the last Ice Age was ending about 10,000 years ago, the River Kennet, which ran through the Gap to join the Thames near the site of the future Pangbourne, suddenly switched its main course and ran through the Coley Gap to join the Thames at its modern confluence.

8. Alder Copse. Alders were a valuable crop and could be grown on land too wet to use for anything else. Ditches have been dug to maintain its wetness. Alder was coppiced – cut off at ground level - and the poles were used, amongst other things, for scaffolding and clog soles. Because it resists rot when kept wet it was used for underwater work. Its charcoal was used to make gunpowder and it provides dyes of several different colours. The London Guild of Dyers used to ceremonially process to Runnymeade to gather alder sap when it started to rise in spring.

9. Riverside fence. This keeps grazing animals away from the river edge and prevents them kicking mud into the water. Layers of silt can kill creatures which rely on clean gravel for habitats and for spawning areas.

10. The medieval road. This insignificant path is all that remains of the original Pangbourne Road.

11. Tidmarsh. The name means 'Tudda's Marsh' and the manor is first recorded (with a vineyard) in 1239 when the 'rent' was the provision of a knight to guard Wallingford Castle for 40 days in time of war.

12. Houses. The ornate cottages were built for the Tidmarsh Estate in about 1830. The first was a Sunday School.

13. The Toll House. This octagonal house was built in the late 18th century to serve the Turnpike Road from

The Toll House at Tidmarsh

Wallingford to Basingstoke. It seems that only the length from Pangbourne to the Great Bath Road at Theale was actually built. In 1832 it collected £83 in tolls.

14. 'The Greyhound'. The existing half timbered house dates from the 16th century but there has probably been an inn on the site for much longer since the site is at the crossing of two important routes.

Tidmarsh Sunday School

15. Mill House. Lytton Strachey, a biographer and member of the famous early 20th century Bloomsbury Group, lived here between 1917 and 1924 principally with the artist Dora Carrington and her husband Ralph Partridge, but also with other lovers, causing a local scandal!

Tidmarsh Mill. A mill is mentioned in 1239. This mill was also owned by the Stone family. They once tried to increase its output by installing new equipment, but when they started it up all the windows fell out! The mill closed in 1937. The green box and solar panel monitors river levels for the Environment Agency.

16. World War 2 'Stop Line'. In 1940 a number of Defence Lines were built across the SE of England. 'GHQ Line Red' ran from the K & A Canal at Theale Mill to the Thames at Pangbourne. It was a wide, deep ditch covered by gun positions. These pill-boxes were designed for a 2 pounder anti-tank gun and light machine guns. The ditch was back-filled after the war.

Tidmarsh Mill

Tidmarsh millstone

17. Oaklands Farm. Is built on an island in the marsh.

18. Alder coppice. Note the massive 'stools' formed by repeated cutting.

19. Peatpits Wood & Sulham Brook. 'Peatpits' probably indicates peat cutting for fuel, although peat was also burned to make potash. The Sulham Brook was probably once a channel of the Kennet.

Alder coppice stools

20. Open hall house. The west end was probably built in the 14th/15th C. with a fire on the floor of a hall open to the roof. The chimney was added later and a floor inserted in the hall.

21. Sulham. The name means 'the farm in a narrow valley'. It is mentioned in Domesday Book and in 1322 had a watermill.

22. Sulham Wood. This ancient beech wood covers a series of very large cultivation

Early house on Sulham Lane

terraces. The dense dog's mercury also shows that it was once cleared land. Pits have been dug into the terraces to provide chalk to lime the fields. There is an excellent view across the Sulham Gap.

23. Wet woodland. This small wood is a SSSI. It is important for its range of wet woodland species.

24. Flood relief scheme. This was built by the Environment Agency to protect the area around Pangbourne School and Kennedy Drive.

25. Railway. Again note the original Brunel bridge and the hart's tongue fern growing in the brickwork.

26. Salteney Mead. This was once Common to Whitchurch, Sulham and Purley and would have been an important source of hay and of grazing. Detached commons provided a resource – hay, firewood etc – for distant

Freshly pollarded willows near Point 26 in 2004

parishes lacking them. The warning sign on the bank marks the outfall of a drain from A.W.R.E. Aldermaston. The pipeline was recently closed down.

Pollard willows. Willows were cut off at about 8 feet above the ground so that the re-growth was out of reach of cattle and horses. This allowed the area to be grazed. Compare the photograph, taken in March 2004 with the present growth. Pollarding extends the life of the tree almost indefinitely. There was a steady demand for willow from thatchers and hurdle makers. Thin strips of willow were even woven into hats. An old willow is second only to an ancient pollard oak as a source of many different habitats for a myriad of creatures from the smallest invertebrates to mammals and birds.

27. Pangbourne Meadow. During both Word Wars troops were trained in building pontoon bridges here. It is now owned by Pangbourne Parish Council and its extension to the south is owned by the National Trust.

28. The Thames Path. Originally a tow path for barges, the path is now a National Long Distance Trail. It runs from Thames Head near Cirencester to the Thames Barrier at Woolwich. Barges were towed by horses and by gangs of men. The men were called 'scufflehunters' from the sound of their feet on the path.

29. Whitchurch Bridge. Built in timber in 1792 to replace a ferry. It was re-built in 1840 and the steel bridge was built in 1901. It is still a privately owned toll bridge.

Sources and further reading

Victoria County History – Berkshire

Morris J (Ed)	*Domesday Book – Berkshire* Phillimore 1979
Ekwall E (Ed)	*The Concise Dictionary of English Place-names* OUP 1974
Mabey R	*Flora Britannica* Chatto & Windus 1997
Williamson T	*Shaping Medieval Landscapes* Windgather Press 2003
Greenaway D & Ward D	*In the Valley of the Pang* The Friends of the Pang, Kennet & Lambourn Valleys 2002
Rackham O	*The History of the Countryside* Dent 1986
Rocque J	*A Survey of the County of Berkshire 1761* reprinted c.1975
Wills II	*Pillboxes. A Study of UK Defences 1940*
	20th Century Defences in Britain Council for British Archaeology 2002
Hogg IV	*The Illustrated Encyclopaedia of Artillery* Guild Publishing London
	Handbook for the Ordnance, O.F. 2-PR., Marks IX and X Land Service. HMSO 1938
Kenneth-Major J (ed)	*Robert Stone Miller of Pangbourne* The International Molinological Society 1980
Phillips D	*The Great Road to Bath* Countryside Books Newbury 1983
Taylor C	*Roads and Tracks of Britain* Dent 1979
Hawkins HL	*On the Former Course of the Kennet between Theale and Pangbourne.* Proceedings of the Geological Association Vol 38 1926

GLOSSARY

AWRE — Atomic Weapons Research Establishment

Bloom of iron — A mass of unrefined wrought iron with large quantities of entrapped slag and voids in the structure. The product of a primitive furnace. Sim D & Ridge 1 *Iron for the Eagles* Tempus Publishing Ltd 2002

Braid — Unrestrained rivers tend to run through a network of channels rather than down a single channel. Such a system is referred to as a 'braided channel' and each individual channel as a 'braid'.

Common — Land owned by one person over which other people (commoners) have defined rights.

Cruck — A curved beam, part of a pair which form an arch, used to support a roof.

Green — A small enclosed area, often created by squatters on manorial waste land.

Jetty — An overhanging upper storey of a house. A common feature of medieval houses.

Leat — An artificial channel conducting water to a water mill, water meadows or other industrial site.

Lye — Potassium hydroxide made by soaking wood ash in water. The water is drawn off as lye.

Lynchet — A terrace along a steep hillside caused by loosened soil moving down slope to collect against a boundary and by loosened soil moving away from the boundary on the other side. The up slope collected soil is called a 'positive lynchet' and the drop on the down slope side is called a 'negative lynchet'. Terraces are often created by ploughing along the contour, in which case they can form a stair-like system. An ancient road running along a slope with arable field on either side can also form a lynchet.

Motte — A large steep-sided mound, originally having a fortification around the top and standing within a fortified enclosure (the bailey). Mainly associated with 11th century Norman occupation.

Pale — A boundary, particularly around a deer park, to contain the animals kept in the park. Typically a high wall or a bank topped with a fence and with a ditch on the inside.

Pightle — A field created by clearing woodland.

Pillow mound — A long low mound covering a network of small tunnels which was built as an artificial rabbit warren.

Podzol — An acid infertile soil caused by rainwater washing chemicals from the upper soils and creating hard layers called pans lower in the structure.

Pound — A fenced paddock with a locked gate within which animals were held when they had been found illegally grazing on a common. The owner could only recover them on payment of a fine.

Pug mill — A mixing machine, usually driven by a horse, in which the clay, sand and chalk were mixed to make the raw material of bricks.

Scufflehunters	The name given to men who towed barges along the River Thames. Said to derive from the noise mad by their feet as they walked.
SSSI	Site of Special Scientific Interest. An area especially designated by law as important for the preservation of particular species of plants, animals and other creatures.
Staddlestone	A mushroom shaped stone used to raise the floor of a building above ground level and to deter rats from entering the building.
Stub	A tree cut off at about 5 feet (1.5m) above the surface and thus neither a coppice stool (cut near ground level), nor a pollard (cut at about 8 feet – 2.5m). Often used as a boundary marker.
Swallow hole	A hole allowing surface water flowing from an impervious surface to penetrate into the underlying strata.

INDEX